A
MILLION TIMES
WE CRY

A
MILLION TIMES
WE CRY

A Memoir of Loss,
Grief, Depression, and
Ultimately Hope

STACEY GRIMES-WEMPE

as told to Mike Wicks

Forefront
BOOKS

Published by Forefront Books, Nashville, Tennessee.
Distributed by Simon & Schuster.

Library of Congress Control Number: 2024911908

Print ISBN: 978-1-63763-207-9
E-book ISBN: 978-1-63763-208-6

Cover Design by Bruce Gore, Gore Studio, Inc.
Interior Design by Mary Susan Oleson, Blu Design Concepts

Printed in the United States of America

To Mom, Dad, and Clinton,
you will live on in my memory forever.
And to my husband, Keith,
and my children, Garrett and Katie.

Contents

Author's Note

I am not a psychologist; neither am I a psychiatrist. My husband and I own a dental practice, where I am the office manager. However, I am a Certified Fearless Living Coach (CFLC)—a program I took to help myself face life after losing my brother to a tragic accident.

I wrote this book first and foremost as a cathartic exercise. I needed to deal with the emotional baggage I had been carrying around with me for decades and to empty my trunk of that baggage. I also wanted my children to know my story and hopefully learn from it so they might be better prepared for the inevitable curveballs life throws at them. The third reason I wrote this book was so that others struggling with their problems might find help in my story of overcoming grief, fear, and anxiety in order to live life more fully and joyfully.

As I began to face the loss, grief, and depression that have been the fabric of my life for as long as I can remember,

I studied how I dealt with the seemingly continual bombard-ment of emotional trauma. The result is *A Million Times We Cry*, a book in two parts: memoir and a short section featuring my observations as a life coach.

My suggestions, advice, and meandering thoughts are based on my personal experiences, not a result of academic study—they come from the heart, tempered by time and reflection. Life teaches you a lot if you are open to listening, so please explore the life coach section at the back of this book and see if any of my advice, suggestions, or points to ponder resonate with you. I wish you well in your journey to better understand the loss, grief, and depression you may be experiencing.

Stacey Wempe
Estevan, Saskatchewan
November, 2023

PART I
My Story

CHAPTER ONE

A Life Frozen in Time

It's April 16, 2020, and the time has come. I'm finally ready. A few days ago, I asked Keith, my husband, to get the box out of storage, and here it is in the garage. Not so much of a box, really; it's more of a chest—a wooden chest about three feet long and two feet wide. It's solid; it looks like it was built to last forever or at least long enough. It's been closed for twenty-three years, since a few days after my brother, Clinton, died in a tragic, horrific accident at the age of twenty-two—an event that haunts me to this day. The chest came into my possession four years ago after my father passed away; my mom originally packed it up, but she passed away eleven years ago, and neither of them ever had the strength to revisit Clinton's life.

Since this box was closed and kept for posterity, I have experienced more emotional pain than any one person should be expected to endure. Today's almost ceremonial opening heralds a new chapter in my life; it's time to move on and share my story. I hope that by sharing what I have learned over the last two decades about grief, loss, and depression, I might make other people's journeys a little easier.

I've never felt brave enough to face rummaging through my brother's worldly possessions—until now. What's changed? I'm still not sure I'm strong enough, but my writing partner, Mike Wicks, suggested it was an essential first step. He was right—it is cathartic, but that doesn't make it hurt any less.

Grief overwhelmed me when Clinton died and then again and again for more than twenty years. I could never make sense of the loss—could never wholly come to terms with it. For a time, I was angry—how could he get up and leave me? How dare he? Then I was numb. The depression came a little later, a bottomless pit into which I crawled more than once.

I was close to my brother; I was only three years older than him, and I always looked out for him. We talked every day. We were a close family; we did everything together, and now it's just me, me and this chest—a coffin for his possessions. Perhaps we should have buried it like a time capsule.

As I lift the lid, the aromatic, woodsy smell of Clinton's favorite cologne, Polo Green by Ralph Lauren, hits me with a tidal wave of nostalgia. At once, I am transported back to when Clinton was twenty-two; at the same time, I feel the urge to turn around to see if he's just walked into the garage to mimic my way of talking, teasing me while laughing uncontrollably. The smell of his cologne—leather, tobacco, earthy, and, yes, overpowering—brings back so many memories. This is hard. I begin to doubt whether I am ready for this. Heck, I always told him he wore too much cologne. The tears stream down my face, and I've not even picked up the stuffie lying on top of everything else. He used to love his stuffie, a cute, white, indeterminate animal, much loved and well-worn. The slightly bedraggled white faux fur brings back memories of a happy prairie childhood.

It's the small things that hit you. Underneath his stuffie, there's a birthday card that opens backward. Our cousin Holly, who was also a lefty, had written in it, "For your birthday. Got you a card designed for lefties." I open the card awkwardly and smile. Then, tears again flow down my cheeks as my hand rests on hundreds of sympathy cards—literally hundreds. Around five hundred people came to his funeral, and the local florists ran out of flowers. Clinton was incredibly popular.

My emotions are frozen in time like the contents of this chest. But I can't staunch the flow of memories—memories that I haven't acknowledged in a long while. Memories of that night, that foggy night. The night that created my personal black hole. Perhaps today will be the day I climb out of it. This is hard, so hard. I miss him so much—my brother, my friend. And I miss my mom and dad because they also left me too soon. Much too soon—I wasn't ready to be left alone.

I gingerly lift a yellowing newspaper, neatly folded, that reads "Memoriams." For the first time, I realize it's an odd word; shouldn't it be *Memorials* or *Obituaries*? Clinton's face smiles back at me, so young and full of unfulfilled promise. The words from the anonymous poem I discovered and placed in the newspaper announcement stare back at me:

You never said I'm leaving.
You never said goodbye.
You were gone before we knew it,
And only God knew why.
A million times we needed you,
A million times we cried,
If love alone could've saved you,
You never would've died.
In life we loved you dearly,
In death we love you still.
In our hearts you hold a place
That no one could ever fill.

It broke our hearts to lose you,
But you didn't go alone,
For part of us went with you
The day God took you home.

We miss him and love him,
and he will always be in our hearts.
Love Mom and Dad, Stacey and Keith

I pick up his Montana State ball cap—he loved Montana. And, oh my God, his Scouts cap. A photo of his best friend, Darryl, who drowned with his father when their canoe overturned in 1991. Another senseless tragedy. Clinton's whole life is here: a class recipe book and a scrapbook biography of Clinton from junior high. Oh my. It was a school project written by Darryl. Two deaths brought into sharp focus.

I've never read the scrapbook biography before; the tears begin to flow again. "Clinton was born in Lampman Union Hospital on September 10th, 1974; he was born about 1 a.m. His parents were Melvyn and Margaret Grimes. He has one sister; her name is Stacey; she has now graduated from Lampman High School and is at Minot University." Several pages later, it ends with the words, "In ten years, Clinton would like to be in Texas on a ranch. In twenty years, he would like to be in Alberta on a ranch and have a good job." I never knew this. This is so hard.

There's another school project tucked away in the chest. In it, Clinton wrote, "My beliefs and values are to have a good life and to be good at things like jobs, and skiing, golfing, and horseback riding. What my family likes about me, I don't know." This makes me laugh out loud for the first time since I opened the box. So many mixed emotions. The teacher had written in red, "You should ask them." He got 52 percent on the assignment. I sift through report cards for every year of school. Teachers liked Clinton, but his academic achievements were average at best—except, of course, when it came to shop; he loved that. Clinton hated school.

A photo of his chipped tooth, music cassettes (the Eagles, Garth Brooks, Reba McEntire), a *Donkey Kong* video game from the '80s, batteries corroded in a remote, a bow and arrows, a skeet shooting trophy—Clinton was good at shooting. Oh, dear Lord, there are receipts, some from the trip we took to Whitefish, Montana, a few weeks before he died: ski rentals, gas, new boots. I look at his signature and remember how hard he tried to make it like Dad's. He loved our father so much. Hidden in his wallet is a photograph of Marsha, his girlfriend at the time of his death, with the inscription "Marsha '97." She was so pretty, and he loved her so much. When I turn it over, I realize that someone, probably my mother, put it here when she closed the chest. It reads, "Mel and Marg, you guys are like my second family, and I hope you always will be. I hope someday the pain will get a little easier, but I'll always be here for you if you need help with anything. Love, Marsha." I put it back into the dark recesses of the wallet, where it belongs, somehow, with him.

I remember his previous long-term girlfriend, Saundra, telling me a story about when they were camping on their way to Whitefish. The campground had a small trout pond, and Clinton was excited to do some fly-fishing. It was a beautiful evening; the sun was setting behind the mountains to the west; it was picture-perfect until Clinton clumsily managed to get a fishhook stuck in his scalp. Saundra told me that he walked over to her embarrassed and wanted her to pull it out, but it was lodged under several layers of skin and she didn't want to look at it, let alone touch it. She was grossed out and tried not to gag. He eventually convinced her to grasp the hook, which was still attached to the line, and said, "For God's sake, just rip it out!" When she hesitated, he whipped his head back and ripped it out himself. She said she almost threw up. That was typical Clinton.

I miss his presence; it's so sad he's not here. I feel a part of me has died. But you can't lock your emotions away; I realize that now. It's what I did for many years, and I was ... I was sick. I was mentally and physically ill because I locked my emotions away and never expressed my feelings. I couldn't admit or share that I wasn't having a good day or that I needed time alone to journal about what I was feeling. That's why opening this chest feels liberating. It feels like I can let my emotions out too—set them free.

April 25, 1997, was like any other day; it was a Friday. My husband, Keith, and I had worked all day, and later we were vegging. I called my brother to see what his plans were for the weekend. Looking back, I must have somehow sensed something was going to happen. I'd felt the urge to tell him how proud I was of him, that I loved him very much, and that I sometimes worried about him because he was a boom truck operator, which is a truck with a crane on it used to move cargo or equipment. I told him what was in my heart. He told me he was the best boom truck operator in southeast Saskatchewan, and there was no need to worry about him. We talked about going to supper and a movie that night but postponed it until the following evening. He said he would pay the bill because Keith and I had just moved into our new house and started new jobs. He asked me if Keith wanted to talk to him, but Keith said not to bother; they'd speak the following day.

It was 5:45 the following morning when my life changed. Someone was knocking at the front door. I remember thinking, *Who the heck could that be?* Keith opened the door, and my aunt and uncle stood there; they told Keith my brother had been in an accident. I was upstairs but could hear some of what was being said. I asked if he was okay. Uncle Darwin replied that no, he was dead. I said, "I just talked to him; how can he be dead?" My mom had asked her brother to come and tell me; he and Aunt Carol lived nearby. I was both hysterical and numb. It's strange what you remember at times like that; I got dressed in red jogging pants, a white shirt, and white shoes. Nothing would ever be the same again. *No, no, no, not my Clinton.*

At 1:00 a.m., just seven hours after I had told him how much I loved him and how proud of him I was, his Chevy Tahoe ran into the twenty-second freight car of a train heading slowly westbound. He had spent the evening with Marsha watching movies, and at close to midnight, she had left to drive home—a journey that would take her over two railway crossings. It was not too foggy at Clinton's house, and so she felt okay to go, even though she was not an experienced driver at only seventeen years old. She crossed the first set of railway tracks close to town without difficulty, but she hit a wall of fog when she reached the second set, four miles from his house. It was so dense that she felt the truck go over the rails but never actually saw them—scary. A few miles later, she couldn't see the road and decided to pull over and call Clinton. Cell reception was usually patchy in that area, but she managed to get through and told him she would turn around and return to his house. Like the knight in shining armor he was, Clinton immediately told her to stay where she was and that he would be there in a few minutes. She waited and waited, but he never showed up. She decided to turn around and head back. A local, Michael James, had passed her a few minutes earlier on his way to town with a friend but was now close to the tracks, heading back in her direction.

The fog was lifting, and she could see Clinton's crumpled truck. Michael said there was no one in it. Marsha screamed that her Clint had to be in there. The windshield was smashed, and the fog swirled around, but as if on cue, it lifted a little more and they could see Clinton lain back in his seat; the airbag had deployed. Marsha shouted to Michael to do CPR because, in her panic, she'd forgotten how, but he slowly shook his head. Later, the police told her that the impact had almost certainly broken Clinton's neck. Visibility was so poor that night that it took the ambulance about an hour to get to Clinton.

Marsha called her dad, whose immediate response was

"What train?" because that track was rarely used. He told her he'd be right there, and in the meantime he told her to call Lionel and his wife, Bev, family friends who lived close by. Marsha was trying to pull Clinton out of his truck when Lionel and Bev showed up. They took her back to their house, and Lionel returned to the crash site with his tractor. Marsha then called my dad, thinking he would come to the house first, but he drove straight to the tracks. Marsha recalls knowing in her heart that Clinton was gone but praying he wasn't. She thought he might have been so cold because it was so cold out.

Later, Marsha was interviewed by the police. She remembers how nice the officer was; he asked her whether she had any questions, and she wondered whether giving Clinton CPR would have helped. The officer gently told her that nothing would have helped.

I always wondered why he didn't hear the train, but fog deadens sound, and he would have had his music playing. Also, the locomotive was a long way away from the twenty-second car. The train driver himself didn't realize there had been a collision. The police had to phone ahead to Carlyle, forty miles away, to stop the train.

Thick fog, an unmarked rail crossing, and terrible timing meant he would never arrive to "save" Marsha. And I would never see my brother again. In an instant, our family crumbled. I was numb—I barely remember the following week. My mother was so angry at Canadian National Railway for not having lights at a crossing known to experience thick fog. Frighteningly, more than two decades later, that crossing still has no lights or barriers; it lies there waiting for its next victim, and the CN corporate giant doesn't seem to care. Yet a few miles away, in Lampman, the lights remain—guarding a crossing that is seldom, if ever, used.

More memories come flooding back. I remember my anger. I was angry, so angry. I was mad at myself for not saving my brother—why couldn't I have said that we should go to the movie tonight, not tomorrow? Then I was angry at Marsha for going out when it was so foggy, and lastly, I was furious at my brother for dying. Years later, my psychologist asked me what I wanted to say to my brother that I didn't get to say. I said, "I am furious at you! You left me. I won't get to talk to you ever again. You won't get to see my kids, and I won't get to see your kids. I won't get to be an auntie to them."

I try to think about all the good times and the incredible conversations, especially the one I had with him just a few hours before he died. I've done a lot of healing between that night and today. I know now that it's okay to revisit that place, stay there for a little while, and cry. It's okay to remember the good times. To look at photos, watch videos, remember.

I refocus, and the chest is empty. Clinton's life is strewn across the garage. It doesn't seem like much, but there is so much life in every item—memories, emotions, things said and things left unsaid. There is healing in this pain. My seventeen-year-old daughter, Katie, has been videotaping this trip back in time so my writing partner, Mike, can understand who Clinton was and what he meant to me—and for me to spend some time remembering my brother. She says, "Mom, that was amazing what you did, honoring Uncle Clinton like that." I hadn't thought of it like that.

I recall asking my therapist about the difference between grief and depression. She said, "Grief usually is two to three months of pure sadness. You ask yourself, *How can I live without this person?* You feel sad; you don't feel whole. You question how you can go on. That is normal, but if it lasts more than a few months, it is important to seek help; you have depression." I remember I cried every day for a year after Clinton died. I was to experience significant loss twice more over the two decades following his death. Grief was to be a frequent visitor, and depression became an unwanted companion for far too long.

Chapter Two

Life in a Small Prairie Town

I was born on October 21, 1971, in Lampman, a small Saskatchewan prairie town twenty miles north of North Dakota. The town was named after the much-celebrated poet Archibald Lampman. He was called the Canadian Keats because he wrote poems celebrating nature. Today, the town boasts a population of 735, but on the day I was born, it was in the region of 650 souls.

We lived in a small house with three bedrooms upstairs and a living room and kitchen downstairs—a typical clapboard house, nothing fancy. It was just a few blocks away from Lampman's four-story hospital. My father, Mel, used to talk about the day of my birth, complaining that he hadn't been allowed in the delivery room. He told a story about the hospital's system for announcing births. Mom was in the final stages of labor, and he was told to go home and look out his bedroom window toward the hospital. Doing as instructed, he said a nurse flashed a light to announce my arrival. He loved that story and laughed every time he told it. I was never sure why they didn't simply use the telephone or, for that matter, why he couldn't have hung out in the waiting room. Perhaps it was his way of saying I was the light of his life!

I was the first granddaughter on my father's side, and my birth was much celebrated. It resulted in me having a special relationship with my dad's family, especially my paternal grandma. I was born with hip dysplasia, a developmental disorder initially undiagnosed. My mother complained to the doctors that something was wrong with me because I would cry a lot, but they couldn't find anything seriously wrong. Several months later, it was diagnosed, and I had to wear leg casts. They weighed about ten pounds each, and a metal bar stuck out from the sides. Mom used to tell me she lost a lot of weight carrying me around and frequently got clonked on the head. However, if it hadn't been for her persistence with the doctors, I wouldn't be able to walk normally today.

My parents were twenty-four when I was born. My mother was striking; my paternal grandfather told my father, "She's a beautiful lady." Mom always dressed well, styling her hair and even wearing makeup to the grocery store. At the same time, she was very down-to-earth. She never sugarcoated things; people always knew where they stood with Margaret. She was also a good cook and loved to entertain. I particularly remember her French bread and Christmas puddings. We called her Saskatchewan's Julia Child because she always cooked with lots of butter and cream. I remember fantastic egg bakes, creamy fish, shrimp, and pasta Alfredo. Clinton liked her turkey, roast potatoes, and Yorkshire pudding dinners—we all did. She made everything from scratch, grew her own herbs, and always bought the freshest ingredients. I remember asking her once how come her chicken was always so tender. Without missing a beat, she replied, "You have to beat the shit out of it with the meat tenderizer." I wonder what Chef Ramsay would say to that.

After she died, people kept coming to me asking for her recipes. I'm sad I didn't learn any of them, because she never wrote them down. How often do we regret the things we fail to do, things that we never felt were important—until they are? I remember the last meal she made, exceptional yet straightforward—lobster with homemade fries. She was very ill, but she needed to cook a final, special dinner for her family.

My grandma Kathleen, my dad's mom, told me Mom hadn't always been such a good cook. Early on in her marriage, there was a time when she called Grandma to ask how to make fried rice. Grandma said, "You just fry it in a pan," thinking it was pretty obvious. A short while later, Mom called back and told her it hadn't cooked. It turned out she hadn't cooked the rice first; she just threw the rice straight from the packet into the pan.

The Grimes Legacy

My family name was Grimes, and we were well-known in our little corner of Saskatchewan. My father worked at the petroleum plant. He was promoted to plant manager at age nineteen, the youngest ever. His father sold farm equipment, including tractors, combine harvesters, and other stuff farmers needed. I remember some of the brands Grandpa sold: Degelman, New Holland, and Versatile. Grimes Sales and Service was very well-known and respected. Dad told me he was put to work tidying the shop when he was only six. Many years later, around the time I was born, Grandpa contracted lung cancer and struggled to manage the business. My dad would work the midnight shift at the plant, go home and sleep for a few hours, and then go to the shop to help Grandpa. Grandpa suffered for five years; Grandma was only in her mid-forties when he died.

Early childhood lessons are important, and I grew up seeing my parents work hard, play hard, and give back to the community. They treated everyone with respect and always put family first. The values we learn or absorb before we are five help determine who and what we are in life. They become deep-rooted in our psyches.

Mom and Dad made a great-looking couple. Like my mom, my dad always dressed well. I have a photograph of him from 1980; he would have been thirty-three, and he was wearing pilot's sunglasses and a jean jacket. He looked so handsome; he was tall and slim back then, but his weight was an ongoing challenge. He had a problematic relationship with food, and his weight would fluctuate a lot during his life, especially during times of stress. Another Grimes trait to which I can all too easily relate.

When Grandpa died, Dad took over the business. I was only nine months old. I wish I could remember Grandpa Grimes. Everyone liked him. He was a pillar of the community for eighteen years and served as mayor of Lampman for fifteen years.

My dad had massive respect for him. When Dad inherited the business, he carried on a long-standing family commitment to the company's twenty or so staff, its customers, and the community. Grandma was the bookkeeper, but my mother gradually took over that responsibility. The company accountant said my mother was probably the best book-keeper he'd ever known. She was amazing; she'd wake up at

5:00 a.m., do the laundry, cook dinner for that evening, and still turn up at the shop in high heels, looking like a million dollars. Unfortunately, neither Clinton nor I inherited her organizational skills.

Dad learned to fly in 1977, which became vital to the business's success. The shop was across the road from Lampman Airport, and he'd often hang out there with his buddies. His customers were spread across Saskatchewan. Whenever they needed an urgent part for a broken-down tractor, he would fly it to them so the machine could be back in service as quickly as possible. Sometimes he would take along a mechanic, and they'd do the repair on the spot. He'd land his Piper Super Cub at a nearby landing strip or right on the customer's farm. By 1983, when he got a bigger Beechcraft V35B Bonanza, he began attaching tiny parachutes to the parts and dropping them from the aircraft. He was known for his pinpoint accuracy; the replacement parts would always land within a few yards of the waving customer. Where many of his competitors had trucks, Dad had his plane. The service side of Grimes Sales and Service had always been important; my dad took it up a notch, and it didn't go unnoticed.

Occasionally, Mom accompanied Dad on his flights, but she didn't enjoy flying. This was especially true after Dad faked a heart attack once in midair. I don't think she ever forgave him for that prank. Clinton and I often flew with him, and I can attest that he was a great pilot.

Clinton was born two years after Grandpa died, on what would have been Grandpa's birthday. Grandpa Grimes was baptized as Clinton, but people always called him Clayton. So my parents named my brother Clinton in honor of Grandpa. When Clinton was born, I was three, and I loved the idea of having a baby brother. It was like having a real live doll. I'd push him around in a red-and-blue pram with daisies painted on it, and I'd help Mom care for him. He had blond hair, blue eyes, and a mischievous smile. We were always close, right from those early days. Even as adults, we'd talk on the phone or see each other almost daily.

We had what most would call a typical prairie life; family was everything. My dad had four siblings who lived close by, and the house was always full of life. Grandma told me she would have liked to have had ten children. We spent a lot of time with Uncle Gary and my Aunts Judy, Barbara, and Karen. Aunt Karen was only nine when Grandpa Clayton died.

Mom loved animals, and we always had pets. When she was younger, she had a billy goat, and Dad bought her a Siamese cat called Missy for their engagement. I couldn't pronounce the cat's name when I was young, and I always called her Sassy; she lived to the ripe old age of eighteen.

Grandpa's and the Grimes family's traits were the topic of many family conversations. One of them was the family's love of television. Back then, televisions were still a luxury item, and Grandpa was one of the first people in Lampman to get one. He had eight of them in his house! This made him very popular; family and friends would regularly drop by to watch TV. My father said that he and Grandpa bonded over movies. By the time I came along, Mom and Dad had several televisions in our house. The trait continues; our place in Estevan, a small city in southeastern Saskatchewan, Canada, less than ten miles from the United States border and twenty-six miles from Lampman, has a television in every room.

The Grimes Sales and Service shop was like a second home when I was growing up. It was just a few doors from our house, but everything in Lampman was close. We could have walked to school, but Mom insisted we take the bus because she said it was a good experience. On the way home, the school bus would always drop us off close to the shop. Rex, our inherited German shepherd, would know when it was time for the bus to arrive and wait for us at the end of the lane. One of Dad's mechanics left Rex behind when he moved on, saying he would return for him. When the mechanic returned six months later, the dog wouldn't go to him; Rex had become part of our family, and my father told the mechanic he couldn't have him back. That dog was remarkable; he would hear Dad's plane coming back from a customer visit and be there waiting at the airport for him when he taxied to the hangar.

A few years later, Dad bought Clinton a Ski-Doo snowmobile, and we'd drive that to school in the winter. Rex would run alongside the Ski-Doo or pull a sleigh with Clinton's friends onboard. Dad would snowblow a lane between the shop and the house to create a track for them. I remember Dad running alongside Clinton, shouting and laughing. Life was simple back then—well, our life, anyway. It revolved around family, friends, community, and the business. So much has changed; life is so much more complicated now.

Mom and Dad did a lot for the Lampman community. They donated to the church and the school and helped wherever they could. Dad would repair whatever needed fixing, and they were both ready volunteers. It goes back to the deep-rooted values by which our family lived. They always donated anonymously, but people knew; it was a small town. On one occasion, Dad donated a pumpjack for a local auction—it was a significant donation. Pumpjacks are used to extract oil from wells where insufficient pressure exists to bring it all to the surface; therefore, a pumpjack was a highly sought after and valuable piece of equipment in Saskatchewan. He regretted his choice later because it was apparent he was the donor. His father had built a legacy around the Grimes name, and my father was honor bound to keep that legacy intact. I remember a guy coming to our door because he had run out of gas; Dad gave him some money so he could make it home. Thirty years later, the man approached my dad at a local event and thanked him. In small communities, small kindnesses are remembered.

After my father died, the local church officials approached me for money to pay for new flooring. They told me that Dad had said he'd be there for them. "Okay," I said, "if Dad said that's what he intended to do, then of course." It's the Grimes way—it's ingrained. I hope my children continue supporting the community, and their children after them. I feel supremely privileged to be financially secure and to have been the beneficiary of my grandparents' and parents' hard work and success. I hope to remain grounded, never forget how lucky I am, and share my good fortune with others.

School Days

I was never keen on school. I wore these glasses with huge frames and thick Coke-bottle lenses, and the other kids would call me four-eyes. I hated those glasses so much. The constant teasing heightened my anxiety so much that I faked being sick so I could avoid school. I also suffered from panic attacks when taking tests and exams. These were early indications of the anxiety and depression that would dog me throughout my life. When you are younger, you just work through it; you are more resilient. I remember writing a report on anxiety and depression for a school project, so I must have known my challenges even back then.

Clinton hated school; he was more of a hands-on kid and was always destined for a career in the trades. Despite my awful glasses and the teasing, I had plenty of friends. We'd ride our bikes around town, go to the outdoor swimming pool, and simply hang out.

When Clinton was six or seven, he teased me mercilessly. He'd steal food off my plate and take my cutlery and hide it; he'd tell me that what I'd ordered at a restaurant was gross and insisted that I'd never have a boyfriend. Although all in good humor, the teasing never stopped, and he and Keith would gang up on me later. He was cheeky to Mom too; he'd smirk and call her by her first name: "Hey, Maggie, what's for dinner?" One of our cousins, Michael, called Clinton's laugh visceral and out of control. As Clinton grew up, having fun became his philosophy for life.

Mom and Dad often had to separate us at the dinner table. On one occasion, I chased him around the house, threatening to hit him with a large piece of firewood. He was an incredibly mischievous kid. He brought Grandma flowers once, which she appreciated—until she discovered they still had their roots attached. He'd yanked them out of her front yard. Come to think of it, on that occasion, I think I was also party to that theft. Then there was the time when he was about thirteen and he and a friend got hold of some gunpowder. He wound up in the hospital with second-degree burns on his face.

Both of my grandmothers were positive influences on me when I was growing up, but I spent a lot of time with Grandma Kathleen when I was young. She lived only five minutes away and liked having me over to her house, especially after Grandpa died. I think I was a welcome distraction. When I was ten or eleven, I remember going to her house every Wednesday; we would cook and watch *Dallas* and *Little House on the Prairie*. Whenever I got mad at Mom and Dad, I would say, "I'm moving to Grandma's house." I lived at her house for a couple of weeks at a time. It was a win-win. Sometimes Mom's depression would descend on her like a dark cloud, and she always refused to see a doctor. When life got too tough for her, it was easier if I went and spent time with Grandma Kathleen. I wonder if sadness can be learned or if it's simply absorbed by osmosis.

Eventually, Grandma remarried, and I got a new grandpa, Grandpa Ben. She was happy in her new marriage, but Grandpa Clayton had been her soulmate, and she would always cry when she talked about him. I think they'd dated since before she was a teen; he'd always taken care of her. I felt I got to know him through her stories, and in turn, I became her emotional support, in a way taking his place. It feels like that was a big part of my childhood. I remember my father saying that I'd helped him look after Grandma. Maybe that was the nascent life coach in me starting to form.

I couldn't grieve for Grandpa Clayton because I'd never known him, but years later, when Clinton died, I could relate to how Grandma must have felt. Later, when I was at college, Clinton's best friend drowned. That was hard, but I felt somewhat distanced from what was happening at home—it didn't affect me as much as if I'd been back in the community. I don't think grief affects you at a primal level until a loved one—someone very close—dies.

When she was in her early twenties, my mom lost her dad, so I never knew either of my grandfathers, which is a shame. But when I was young, I visited my maternal grandmother occasionally. She lived in Estevan, and I remember visiting her, watching soaps on television, and reading the *National Enquirer*. It's strange what you remember. Mundane activities in many ways, but remembering them brings waves of nostalgia.

Mom and Dad attended every school event and parent-teacher evening. They were hands-on; Dad would be one of the only fathers to make an appearance. They never missed a concert, play, sporting event, or any other activity in which Clinton and I were involved.

We used to call Dad "Dr. Phil" because everyone went to him for advice. He was a great listener and was always supportive. Mom told me that whenever they went to a wedding or a big event, he would never get a chance to sit down; people would gravitate toward him, and he'd be the center of attention. That was why he was such a great salesman; people liked and trusted him—he could sell anything.

My parents often won vacations in contests run by the company's suppliers. This meant they were very well-traveled. I remember them going to Jamaica, Mexico, Las Vegas, and other exotic places. Sometimes Clinton and I would go with them. My friends were always amazed that we went on so many vacations. It wasn't as common in those days. I remember family ski trips to Banff and Steamboat Springs in Colorado. In grade two, we went to Florida; that was our first big family trip. My friends would say, "Oh, I wish I could be adopted into your family. You guys travel so much."

On vacation, Clinton was a wild card; when he was about ten he'd do cannonballs into the pool to splash young women sunbathing, and in the ocean he would pretend to be a fish and flap his fins in people's faces. He was intent on getting a reaction, but he was so cute with his blond hair and blue eyes that no one could be mad at him for long—and his mischievous smirk defused any situation. My parents bought a cabin on Boundary Dam Reservoir, close to Estevan. It's where Clinton and I learned to water-ski. The cabin wasn't large, but it was always filled with family and friends. We often had twenty to thirty people visiting at a time—aunts, uncles, cousins, and friends would just turn up and hang out. One year, Dad bought a houseboat and renovated it. In winter, we'd ice fish. When I was about eleven, Dad built me a tiny cabin, a cedar log house. It had bunk beds, and my friends would stay over and we'd listen to music. These were good times. I guess I was spoiled—my parents gave me almost anything I wanted. Despite being financially comfortable, my parents led simple, unpretentious lives and were stalwart and generous community members.

All good things come to an end, though; it was tough on Mom trying to keep up with two homes. After Mom died and Dad became ill, he often wondered why people didn't pop by anymore. I told him things had changed, that it was different now. When Mom died, the energy died with her to a certain extent. But all that came later.

I may have been spoiled, but I was expected to contribute

and "know the value of a dollar," as my father used to say. In grade six or seven, I would help out at the shop, babysit, and cook family meals. Later, during high school, I worked as a receptionist at the local Shand Power Station during summer breaks. I always did something. Having a work ethic was important to our family; no one got a free ride. People respected our family and never begrudged our lifestyle—the community knew it was hard-earned.

In 1984, Dad went into partnership with a cousin, Paul Grimes. The company was called Southern Resources; it was a young oil company based in southeastern Saskatchewan. By 1989, Dad was no longer selling farm implements, but he kept farming. He loved sowing, watching things grow, and then reaping the rewards. Years later, he took over the company and became the sole owner. The business went on to become quite the success story. One of Dad's good customers, Paul Cheung, sourced a more efficient pumpjack from China, the HG pumpjack. It had a unique, odd design, featuring a curved walking beam that used two counterweights instead of one. It was a significant advance in energy-efficient pump-jack technology. Instead of losing a customer, Dad partnered with Paul and began importing this newfangled piece of machinery. Dad's obituary in *Pipeline News* stated, "The HG pumpjack changed the landscape of Saskatchewan."

The new design took off so much that Dad and his new partner invested in the manufacturing company. In their best year, they sold almost 1,500 units; you couldn't drive far in our part of Saskatchewan without seeing one in a field. They sold over fourteen thousand units locally and to oil companies in Alberta, Manitoba, Utah, and North Dakota. In 2001, Keith and I visited the factory in China with Dad and Paul. It was the New Year, and they threw us a big party. We felt like celebrities.

When I was around fifteen, I started noticing boys, or maybe they started noticing me, and my father said, "You're at that boy-crazy age." I'd always been a reliable, responsible child, but then I lied to my parents one day. I told them I was going to the movie theater, but I was going to a friend's house and hanging out at the 7-Eleven store. Clinton knew where I was, and he told Grandma. My dad came looking for me, and he was mad. I felt awful. I remember thinking, "Oh my God. I am in such big trouble." At the time, I had my own phone line in my bedroom—yes, I was spoiled— and Dad took it away. I was devasted, but after a few days, I simply used the family phone to talk to all my friends—for hours. After a week of having people calling and being unable to get through to my father, he relented and reinstalled my "private" line. I don't think it resulted from losing my phone privileges, but I never did anything like that again. The worst punishment was to see my father furious, disappointed, and not wanting to talk to me.

Clinton was always snooping in my room, and when he was about eleven, he found some Maxi Pads in one of my drawers. "Hey sis, what are these for?" I got flustered and told him they were to prevent sweaty armpits. He laughed, but the look on his face told me he knew exactly their purpose.

I suppose, in some ways, it sounds like an idyllic childhood. It was, but it wasn't all smooth sailing. It was tough for my parents to run a business in the '70s and '80s and work side by side every day. They farmed and ran the busy pumpjack business—there was always so much work. And, of course, as with all companies, there were financial stresses.

I remember seeing Mom hyperventilating once, blowing into a paper bag during an anxiety attack. She was very self-critical. She would say she was fat, ugly, and not smart enough. Of course, none of that was true; it was just her perception. To the outside world, her work was impeccable, and she had a successful life. She was a perfectionist, which is always a problem because things are rarely perfect. A wise person once said perfect is the enemy of good. Work became all-consuming for a time, and she would sometimes shut family out and, in practical terms, self-isolate. Paradoxically, when family, customers, employees, or someone in the community needed help, she'd immediately be there for them.

Life is not about what happens to us and the scars that traumatic events leave behind; it's how we deal with those events and move on with our lives. I had an incredibly fortunate, some might say privileged, childhood. Still, looking back on those days, I suffered from undiagnosed anxiety, and there were early indications that depression would become a permanent shadow in my life. Like everyone, I experienced loss. I lost grandparents, my parents lost friends, our pastor passed away, and several close friends died, some tragically. I knew about death, but it wasn't until later that I felt the true intimacy of loss and grief. With loss, there is no one-size-fits-all type, and not all grief is equal. Now, I look back at my life and can identify those moments in time, those incidents that were detrimental to my mental health. I realize that, in most cases, I did not fully process what happened or address my feelings surrounding those events. I remember struggling with emotions when I was young. They are messy and difficult to deal with; what do you do with them? They make you cry, and they just get in the way. So, I decided to ignore them and deal with them later. Of course, they built up until I couldn't cope, and eventually, the dam burst. My wedding, for instance, brought out the worst in me.

CHAPTER THREE

A Marriage Proposal

In the fall of 1989, I started at Minot State University in North Dakota. Minot is known as the Magic City. Going to college in the States may sound daring for a prairie girl, but it's only a two-hour drive from Lampman. I decided to focus on speech pathology and undertake a bachelor of science in communication disorders. My mother came with me to help me choose my electives and was adamant that I learn Spanish. I told her there was no way I would take Spanish, and we ended up having words. And my words were not too ladylike. That's when I met Karla, whose father had also accompanied her to "help" choose an elective. They, too, argued about classes, but when she discovered what I had said to my mother, she said, "Oh, I could never say that to my father." We both laughed, but I felt a little guilty. Our parents had stormed off, and we could see them smoking outside, probably telling each other they should never have come in the first place and that we were ungrateful girls. I lived in residences for the first year to meet people, make friends, and socialize. Karla was in the next room, and we became best buddies.

After graduating from high school, I'd returned to work at the power station and continued through the first summer of university. I was nineteen and soon discovered that tragedy lurks at the edges and in the shadows of our lives. May 25, 1990, started like any other day. The power station was under construction. It was extremely windy, and I remember being concerned about the boom on the crane working close to the trailers we were using as offices and a cafeteria. A short time later, I talked to an engineer about how windy it was outside, and then, switching gears, we started discussing our weekend plans. I told him excitedly about my upcoming family trip to Minot. We were interrupted by an enormous crash, and it became dark, as if the sun had gone behind a cloud. All I could see out of the window was a wall of dust. The engineer ran outside. Within seconds he was back, yelling for me to call 911. A sixty-five-ton crane had fallen back onto the trailer housing the cafeteria. It was 10:10 a.m., and many workers were on their coffee break.

The local radio announced the accident shortly afterward, and the phones started ringing off the hook within minutes. The first caller was my father. I remember him saying, "I've never been so happy to hear your voice." After assuring him I was safe, I was inundated with calls from people asking after loved ones. It was tough. My boss instructed me not to provide any details; not that we had any—it was chaos initially. I dealt with the constant stream of inquiries as best I could. Two people died that day, and six others were seriously injured. It could have been me. It almost was. I was numb at the time. I just did as I was told. I answered the phone, deflecting questions as instructed. I went through the motions.

The company offered counseling to employees; I went to one session. I should have gone to more. It's only thirty years later that I realize how valuable it would have been— it's only now that I have begun to recognize the impact that day had on me. I didn't lose a loved one, but death had paid a close visit, and perhaps I lost a slice of my innocence that day. Life can be cruel; it can be random. I never processed the events of that day or my feelings. I shrugged them off, or at least I thought I had. In reality, I buried them to be dealt with later, like so much of life's other baggage. Maybe it was a simple coincidence or some weird foreshadowing, but one of the people who died was named Clint. It was my last summer at the power station.

Receiving a Ring

Back at university, I worked hard but found it tough going. The saving grace was that I loved university life—the socializing, the wide circle of friends, and the feeling of being grown-up and independent. My grades weren't that good, but they were good enough to keep me in school. I headed home twice a month, more often if there was a special occasion happening at home. In my second year of college, I moved into my own apartment, which felt very adult.

The second week of July 1992, when I was back in Lampman, Keith proposed. It wasn't a surprise; we'd been together for five years, and I knew it was coming; we'd discussed marriage often—it was our destiny. I'd met him at a New Year's party. I was in eleventh grade; we had just returned from a Montana ski trip, and I hadn't planned on going out, but a friend called, and my dad encouraged me to go and have some fun. We connected immediately. It sounds calculating, but he ticked all the boxes on my criteria list for a serious relationship. He was going to college; he had a career in dentistry mapped out, knew exactly how his life would pan out, and was charming and handsome. What more could I ask for?

When I was young, my best friend Karyse and I talked about our wedding days, what married life would be like, and how we would be there for each other. I wanted to be a teacher or a nurse and have two children, a boy and a girl. My dad called that "the million-dollar family"—one of each. I also said I wanted my wedding and reception on some acreage. It's funny; almost everything I said to Karyse that day came true.

Later in July, Keith and I decided to collect the ring. Keith had put it on layaway at a jeweler in Minot. I was still attending Minot University, so we planned to stay at my apartment there. Initially, it would be just Keith and me, a mini romantic getaway, but Mom invited herself to come along.

Mom always did so much for everyone else; she rarely asked for anything for herself, so I didn't have the heart to refuse when she asked to accompany us to pick up the ring. In the end, it was an excellent opportunity to bond with her. We went out for supper; she told us she was proud of us and couldn't wait for the wedding. Mom was a lot of fun, and it was a blessing to have her involved in the planning. She never pushed her ideas on us; it was always about what we wanted and how she could help make it happen. During our stay in Minot, we decided to have the wedding at the family farm, in a big tent, not in a church. We picked up the ring. It was a solitaire half-carat diamond on a gold band. Mom was a jewelry fashionista, so she probably thought it was plain, but I loved its simplicity. I'm glad she came. None of us know how long we have left with our parents; they often leave us too early.

Becoming a "Failure"

The following year, I graduated. Unfortunately, during the time it took for me to get my undergraduate degree, the entry criteria for becoming a speech pathologist had changed and now a master's degree was required. My grades weren't good enough to get me into the master's program. I remember the rejection letters—eleven of them, each one a dagger to my heart telling me I wasn't smart enough, worthy enough. I felt useless—a failure. I remember calling my dad and bawling over the phone. He dropped everything and came to support me.

Not getting into grad school was a massive blow, but Keith and my family were there for me—they were my rock. Unfortunately, their support didn't help me overcome a feeling of abject failure. I felt useless, good for nothing. Mom and Dad sat me down one afternoon on the couch and told me it was okay. Mom held my hand, and Dad sat nervously, unsure what he could say to help. A Grandma saying was dusted off: "Nobody can take away your education," a truism that means nothing, but it helped comfort me a little at the time.

I returned to Saskatchewan and, in 1993, volunteered at a day hospital in Estevan, helping elderly and frail outpatients as a speech and recreation aid. I embraced this temporary assignment and got my family involved. I convinced Keith to dress up as Santa at Christmas, and Mom came and played the piano when we played musical bingo. She once asked me, "Stacey, why are you always yelling at your clients?"

I looked at her and said, "Mom, they're all deaf; they can't hear me unless I yell."

She looked at me for a few seconds as if she were thinking of a comeback and then said, "Good point."

It was good to be living in Lampman with Mom and Dad—it was my safe place. Keith was always part of the Grimes family.

Mom and Dad gave me a unique perspective on life that permitted me to change course when life threw barriers in my way.

My volunteer work helped me get a job as a recreational therapist covering maternity leave. They were happy days; I enjoyed working with older adults. The following year I worked for an oil company for a while. During this period, however, my anxiety was full-blown. I felt my life falling apart. My self-confidence was nonexistent. The voice in my head—that ongoing background narrative we all have—told me all sorts of negative stuff. The lies seemed real enough, as they always do at the time. It kept telling me this was the end of my life. Heartbreaking, maybe, but the end of the world? The stories we tell ourselves.

Dad calmed me down and helped me come up with a new plan. He suggested I become a dental assistant and work in dentistry with Keith. I remember telling him it was a dumb idea, but he looked sternly at me, pointed his finger, and said, "Missy, you think about it!"

I stewed on it for a year and ended up taking his advice.

CHAPTER FOUR

A Saskatchewan Wedding

When planning the wedding, my mom's love of the British Royal Family and mine for Lady Diana dominated our thinking. On July 29, 1981, I'd gotten up at 4:00 a.m. to watch Diana marry Prince Charles, and I was entranced. Fourteen years later, I got our local florist to replicate Lady Di's bouquet. My wedding dress was a tribute to the one Elizabeth and David Emanuel had created for Diana. The bouquet was crammed with white roses and lilies and weighed a ton. The dress was very "poofy" but, at the same time, elegant and classy. I felt like a princess. My mom and I planned the wedding together, and it was another opportunity to bond. It was my father, though, who took my bridesmaids and me to Minot so they could choose their dresses. We all piled into the motorhome for the journey—dress-shopping, Saskatchewan style.

During the lead-up to the wedding, I was, I must admit, a bridezilla. The stress I'd been suffering, the feelings I'd been suppressing, all came to the surface. I was impatient and snarky if things weren't done immediately and exactly my way. Without question, I handled the wedding stress poorly—and that's probably an understatement; I could have been on one of those television programs about wedding divas. I still feel sorry for Karyse, who was my maid of honor. I fretted about everything, even things out of my control, such as the weather. I felt it had to be the perfect day; I had sky-high expectations of myself and everyone involved in the planning. A perfect storm of emotions fueled my anxiety and depression—I was psychologically and physically spent by my wedding day. I had nothing left to give; even smiling took too much energy. I knew I wasn't in a good mental state, but I kept telling myself I'd deal with it later. Fear feeds procrastination, and I had them both by the bucketload.

We got married on July 8, 1995. We'd initially planned a church wedding with all the pomp and circumstance and a two-hour ceremony, but there were too many rules. It felt like it was someone else's tradition and expectations, not ours. I vetoed that idea and channeled the child that had dreamed of her wedding day all those years ago with Karyse. I demanded—yes, demanded—a wedding at the farm, on acreage. In the end, Keith and I did it our way, or mostly my way, and my parents were supportive.

Princess Diana Meets National Lampoon

The day started in a similar vein to a *National Lampoon* movie. Three to four hundred people attended, some arriving early in the day in their motorhomes. I remember one of my uncles jokingly asking my father if he could dump his sewage in the yard. We'd created a fairy-tale setting with a giant red-and-white-striped tent; my bridesmaids were in dark red. I wore my stunning white dress and carried a princess's bouquet; my hair was up, and my makeup was perfect. Clinton worked tirelessly to make sure everything was ready for my big day. He set up tables and chairs, ensured the sound system worked, and marshalled the cars and RVs as they arrived. He was the perfect foreman for the event.

Everyone had fun; the videographer said it was the most fun wedding he'd ever filmed. Somebody suggested that people sing instead of tapping their glasses to make the bride and groom kiss. I remember my bridesmaids, including Keith's young sister, singing, "Love and marriage, love and marriage, go together like a horse and carriage."

Keith's uncle was hilarious as master of ceremonies. He said, "Dentists are the only men who can tell a woman when to open and close her mouth and get away with it." I'm not sure that joke would go over as well today—although maybe it would work in rural Saskatchewan. He also told my parents, "Don't think of it as losing a daughter; think of it as gaining a bathroom." He set the tone for the wedding.

The ceremony was beautiful; my cousin Darren, a missionary in Africa, officiated. He'd made the long journey especially to be there for us on our special day. The love in the tent was palpable; it was a huge family event. Everyone on both sides came—several generations under one roof, or in this case, tent. Unbeknownst to everybody, it was the last family gathering Clinton would attend.

I look like the epitome of a happy young bride in my wedding photographs. My wedding video, however, tells a different story. The camera rarely catches me smiling in the video footage unless I knew it was pointed in my direction. People often ask why I didn't smile more. There's no easy answer, or at least one that doesn't involve a therapist's opinion. My anxiety got the better of me, and the best way I can explain it is that I was MIA, missing in action. The stress built up to a level where I became an automaton.

It rained the weekend before the wedding, and we had no backup plan. We managed to erect tents two days before the wedding, but I wasn't sleeping, worrying about whether the weather would ruin my special day. Or I'd fret about anything else my imagination could conjure up. It was a wonderful day; I just wish I could have been more present.

A Honeymoon with Family and Friends

We drove our camper to Alberta for our honeymoon. I slept all the way; I was exhausted. I remember Keith asking me how much sleep I needed. Anxiety was my constant companion, and it wore me down. The only time I seemed to keep my anxiety at bay or was able to subdue it was when I was in nature. Camping was a Grimes family tradition. We all loved it; it was a great way to see the country and let loose—we worked hard and played even harder.

Keith and I went to Banff National Park and hiked about four miles to the crystal clear, aquamarine-colored pools called the Ink Pots. We passed two stunning waterfalls and walked along catwalks hanging over the canyon's edge. The pools themselves are situated in a meadow above Johnston Creek. They get their name from the little blots at the bottom of each pool from which the water bubbles up.

Being out in the countryside, I felt like a huge weight had been lifted from my shoulders. I was in awe of the scenery. Sitting around a campfire at night telling stories, reminiscing, and eating simple food cooked well, all against a backdrop of mountains and the distant sounds of nature, was heaven to me. My anxiety disappears when the air is clean and crisp and I see the mountains. Being outdoors, away from everything, is good for my soul—it renews, reenergizes, and calms me.

It may seem strange to some people that we chose to visit friends and family during our honeymoon. But family is important to both Keith and me; in fact, it is everything. We saw my Aunt Bev; Uncle Gary (my father's brother); cousins Kirk and Kevin; and their wives, Deb and Rhonda, in Edmonton. We went to the Calgary Stampede, and I met up with my bridesmaid Trina, who lived in Calgary. It was my first time at the Stampede, and I was blown away by how much was going on, from chuck wagon races, bull riding, and barrel racing to an entire fairground with a Ferris wheel and several dozen rides and booths. Heck, even Mickey and Minnie Mouse were there as parade marshals. It was a fun honeymoon, and I was glad to get away after the stress of planning the *big* wedding. I've learned that I can work extremely hard for an extended period, but then I must get away and recuperate. My dad could always tell when I was suffering from burnout. He'd looked at me squarely and say, "Stacey. You need to get away—now."

CHAPTER FIVE

Life Is Not a Straight Line

In September 1995, I went to Regina, the capital of Saskatchewan and about two hours northwest of Lampman, to take my dental assistant program. I lived with Aunt Judy (my father's sister) and Uncle Bob for eight months. Every weekend I'd drive to Saskatoon to be with Keith. He helped me study, and work on my hand-eye coordination. I ended up being complimented by my instructor on how much I excelled in this area. However, I didn't do well in other parts of the course, and my marks weren't the greatest. Dad always encouraged me by saying that as long as I tried my best, that was all he could ask; he reiterated that he and Mom were proud of me. I'm tenacious, and I did study hard, but I found it challenging at the time.

Initially, I applied for the dental hygienist program but wasn't accepted. Later, my instructors asked why I didn't reapply. I can't remember what I told them, but the truth was I lacked confidence; I just didn't believe I was smart enough. Back then, as they still are, my family was everything to me, and the need to be close to them and, of course, to my new husband was overwhelming. It was far more important than career ambition.

I graduated in May 1996 and went home to Estevan. We had rented an apartment there because Keith was going to do his practicum with Dr. Blue and I was going to be Keith's dental assistant for the summer. Dr. Blue had been our family dentist for years. Keith had initially connected with Dr. Blue at a high school career day, and he knew Keith had always wanted to be a dentist. They'd kept in touch, and Keith was thrilled when Dr. Blue asked him to come and work as an associate in his practice once he graduated.

The summer of '96 was terrific; Keith and I worked side by side at the clinic. I enjoyed being his assistant. Once the practicum was over, we returned to Saskatoon so Keith could do his final year at dental school. I managed to get a job as a dental receptionist in a downtown clinic. Times were good; we lived in Keith's Uncle Murray's basement, and our social life ramped up with concerts, parties, restaurants, movies, and everything else twentysomethings get up to before life becomes serious.

As summer turned to fall, I got laid off but immediately got receptionist work at a temp agency. I enjoyed the diversity of the work and meeting new people. I worked at a Coca-Cola plant, a company that made fertilizer, and a TV station. I never knew from week to week where I'd be working; it was a lot of fun.

The rest of the year went by in a blur; we enjoyed living in Saskatoon and went home to Estevan for Christmas and, whenever we could manage it, for a long weekend. In February, Keith took off to do his month-long practicum. He chose to do it in Fond du Lac, a Dene First Nation settlement. It is a remote, fly-in community of about 850 people on Lake Athabasca, surrounded by forest in the far north of Saskatchewan. Access to dental care in such small, isolated communities is usually poor, and Keith was proud that he could go and help out. When he returned, he was pumped and said it was an experience he would never forget.

With Keith away, I decided to move home, prepare for my new job as a receptionist at Dr. Blue's clinic, and prepare our new house for Keith's return. I'd also be less of a distraction for Keith while he studied for his finals.

We'd found our new home earlier in the year after a relatively short search, which was surprising given the tight geographical area we were willing to consider. Mom came with us to look at houses with the realtor. She was hilarious and kept coming out with what we called her "funnyisms," such as calling ugly houses "kitty-dishes." After looking at fifteen properties, we found the "homey house" we were looking for and ended up living there for twenty years and raising two children—we loved it.

I started with Dr. Blue in April 1997, and Keith joined as an associate a month later. At Easter, Mom, Dad, Clinton, Marsha, and I went to our family condo in Whitefish for a weeklong vacation—poor Keith was stuck in Saskatoon studying. Whitefish is a small town of around 7,700 set in the Rocky Mountains. The mountain resort is a fantastic place to ski and mountain bike. It was one of the best holidays we ever had as a family.

Of course, none of us knew it would be the last. My apology for aphorisms, but life can turn on a dime, fate can be a fickle friend, and life is too short not to live it to the fullest. My mom and dad were probably the happiest I'd seen them for a long time. Clinton and his new girlfriend, Marsha, were in love, discussing graduation and their future life together. Marsha was only seventeen, but the four-year difference bothered no one—they were a match made in heaven. However, in a prescient moment, he had told his close friend Kirby, Keith's brother, "If anything happens to me, make sure you look after my princess."

Grandpa Clayton's family

Grandma Kathleen and her sisters

Grandpa and Grandma Grimes getting married

Auntie Judy, Dad, and Uncle Gary

Grandma Freda when
she was younger

Dad and Uncle Gary

Mom and her family
when she was little

Mom and her sisters

This is the most beautiful
picture of Mom

Mom won the figure
skating carnival and was
named Ice Princess—she
loved being at the rink

Mom's family picture

Dad's family picture

Top: Grandpa Rudy walking Mom down the aisle
Above: Mom and Dad—just married

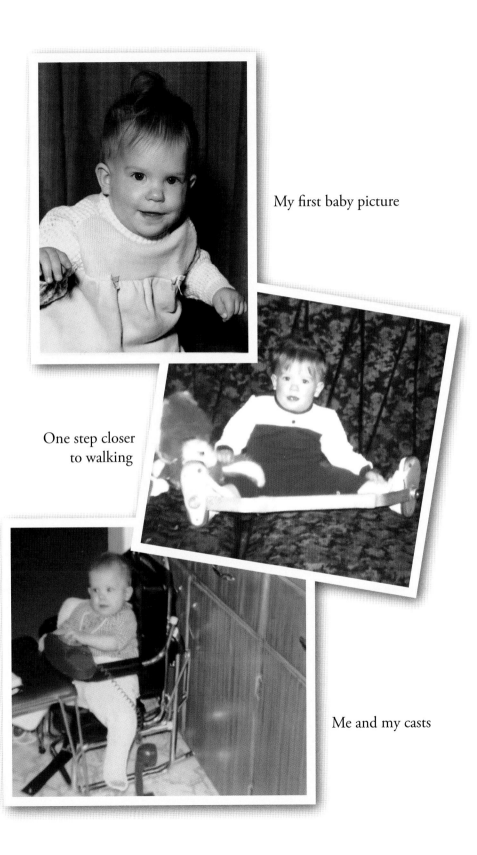

My first baby picture

One step closer
to walking

Me and my casts

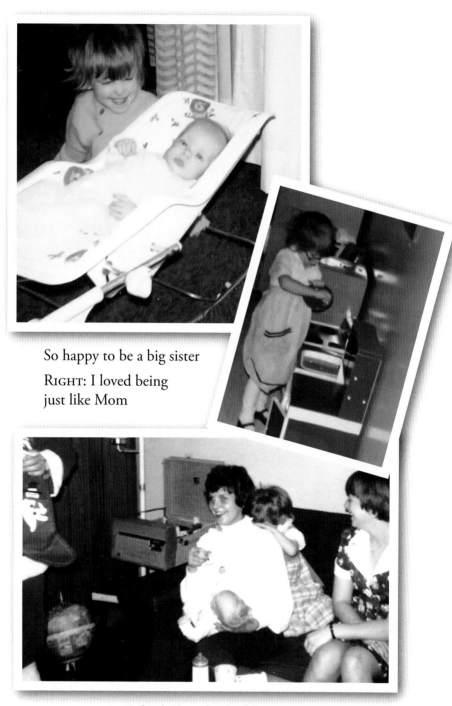

So happy to be a big sister
RIGHT: I loved being
just like Mom

I think I'm afraid of Santa

Family picture

Clinton on the phone

Clinton trying on
Dad's cool shades

Getting ready for bed with Sassy the cat

Pushing Clinton around like a doll

Dad and Clinton

At the parade in Lampman

We love parades

Clinton driving his Kitty Kat Skidoo

Dad and Clinton loved airplanes

Clinton and I
at our cousin's
birthday

Clinton
taking time
out of playing
video games
for a photo

We had burgers at Clinton's favorite restaurant, the Bulldog Saloon, a noisy, fun sports bar, and then we found a great tavern called Casey's that had a great atmosphere. It was in a heritage building, home to saloons and billiard halls for over a century. The place was bustling, and Clinton became reflective. He said he was missing Keith, who was like a brother to him, and couldn't wait for him to come home. We talked about our new house, and Clinton said, quite romantically, I thought, that he and Marsha were set for life.

He had a wonderful log cabin a few blocks from Mom and Dad's and a great job in the family business, and his big sister's house was only a short drive away. We all felt we had won life's lottery—we had it all, or so we thought. I wish I could freeze that moment and replay it repeatedly—my own Groundhog Day. I'd give anything to live it again—that moment when all our lives were filled with endless possibilities. Of course, not all possibilities are endless, as we would soon discover.

I was living with Mom and Dad, excitedly counting down the days until Keith and I moved into our new house. Keith was still in Saskatoon, and even though we'd only been back a week from Whitefish, Mom and Dad had gone on another trip to California. I invited Clinton over for dinner and was cooking burgers for us when the phone rang. Clinton answered it; it was Dad. After chatting for a while, it was

65

apparent that Dad had asked Clinton what his sister was cooking for dinner. Clinton looked over at the stove and said, "Looks like cow patties to me." I knew he wasn't referring to beef by the smirk on his face. I told him I didn't have to cook for him if he felt that way. We laughed; it was all part of how we ragged on each other—small, intimate moments of family life that are easily taken for granted but which are enshrined in my memory forever. Oh, and the burgers? They were great!

On Friday, April 25, Keith and I moved into our new house. Typical of our family, Clinton, Mom, and Dad all pitched in to help; we didn't have much furniture, but it felt good to have everyone involved. It was the next day, early in the morning, when Clinton died. I remember it clearly. I remember going to work and looking forward to the weekend, especially watching a movie with Clinton on Saturday. It had been a hectic week, and we were all looking forward to a relaxing weekend. Mom and Dad drove to the casino at Kenosee Lake; it was a pleasant drive, and Dad loved casinos. They would forever regret not asking Clinton to go with them, but you can't go back and change fate. Clinton was in a very upbeat mood that evening and called a lot of people, touching base and chatting. I was one of those people, and our conversation was somewhat unusual. As I mentioned in chapter one, I had felt an urgent need to tell him how much I loved him, what he meant to me, and how proud his big sister was of him. After I got off the phone, I felt a sense of completeness. It was as if I had accomplished something important in my life. I was the person my parents had hoped I'd be—kind, respectful, loving. I looked forward to supper with him and Marsha the next day before the show. I never dreamed it would be the last time I spoke to him.

Clinton's Death

The following day, Saturday, April 26, 1997, the day of the accident, was the worst day of my life, and its effect on me will live with me forever. No one prepares you for the overwhelming, all-encompassing grief of losing a loved one. Looking back, I would have done so many things differently. David Zindell, the author of the science fiction novel *The Broken God*, wrote, "Before, you are wise; after, you are wise. In between, you are otherwise." After Clinton's death, it took me a long time to become wise, and that was only after many years of reading books about loss, grief, and depression.

I remember, in the immediate aftermath of the tragedy, being in shock. I had no idea what to do. What was I supposed to do? What was expected of me? I grasped that Clinton was dead, but I didn't want it to be true; I didn't want to believe it because believing it would make it true. How could it be so?

I had talked to him only a few hours previously. It must be a mistake. That's denial—denial in the face of the facts. Then came the despair, sadness, and anger—and then all three simultaneously in a slightly different form: pain, distress, and immense sadness—the unholy trinity. Despair hit me immediately. I thought, *How can I live without him?* Twenty-two years. We were blood: the good, sad, and incredibly happy times. Everything we ever did together was there in my mind; I conjured up vivid images of him in what I call "memory pictures." Often they came unheeded. Now they are frozen in time, a celluloid end of film thwacking against the spinning reel of a silent and dark projector.

I've learned that grief never leaves; it remains an unwanted guest. Whatever anyone might tell you, you never get over it. Your life is changed forever. Something died in me the day Clinton hit that train. The pain and despair, however, ease over the years. The intensity lessens gradually, almost imperceptibly, and you look at grief and loss through a different lens.

I was stuck in immediate grief for a long time, thinking of *how* Clinton died rather than his positive impact on my life. I should have focused more on which of his incredible qualities I wanted to preserve. Which did I want to adopt or pass on to my children? Memories became locked in a vault in my mind, and I couldn't decide which, if any, I wanted to let out. I realize now that I should have sought help. I cried constantly. I recognized I was depressed, not just naturally distraught, which was something.

The phone calls from well-wishers didn't help—calls from people who hadn't heard that Clinton had passed or had only just heard. I couldn't sleep. I took a sedative, Ativan, and so did Mom and Marsha.

Mom and Dad reacted very differently to Clinton's death. Dad clammed up; Mom wanted to talk about her "sonny-bunny." The contrast was eerie and unsettling, like the first time I walked into our church after the accident and everybody stared. Going back to work was traumatic for Mom and Dad. Clinton's office, desk, and possessions were frozen in time as if simply waiting for him to return from a vacation.

Dear God, how will I get through this?—I need to be strong for my parents. The strange thing is, to this day, I have no clear idea of what a strong me looks or feels like. However, I held my sadness and depression at bay for my parents. I put my worry on hold.

The funeral, which was held at the aptly named Our Lady of Seven Sorrows, was a big affair. The community came out to support us; our extended family was a lifeline to sanity, and our work family stood firm. The support we got from everyone was a tribute to the Grimes family name and our contributions to the community.

My biggest regret from that period was that I didn't write a eulogy for my brother. At the time, my pain and despair wouldn't let me reach down into myself and go to that place where I would have had to directly confront my innermost feelings. Life goes on for everyone else, in one way or another, but when someone at church or at home would tell a favorite joke of Clinton's or share a funny story about him to try to make me laugh, it would send me into a spiral of anger. *What the hell were they thinking? How could they be happy and laughing like nothing had happened, that some small part of our world hadn't been ripped away?*

I learned later that Marsha had reacted the same way. She said she used to think, *How can you be laughing and having fun?* She told me that, for several years, she couldn't cope with people laughing or having fun on the anniversary of Clinton's death. To this day, she finds the anniversary very difficult. Often, it's an unconscious feeling of sadness, and then she realizes it's that time.

It took me years to process my brother's death. And yes, I learned that laughter is the best medicine and that we need it to feed our souls, but it was all too raw back then. I wasn't ready. Not by a long shot. The pain and distress one feels at losing someone relates to your love for them, and I loved Clinton with all my heart and soul. He was my brother. He was my friend. He was part of me.

I wish I had known what grief looked like before it hit me. At the time of Clinton's death, I'd never heard of grief cycles.

But I know that my first stage of grief was *numb*, or perhaps a better description would be *zombie*. My ups and downs were unpredictable. Early on, my lows lasted for days, sometimes months. Google *grief*, and you will come up with thousands of articles and illustrations of grief wheels and the stages of grief. The Swiss-American psychiatrist Elisabeth Kübler-Ross named five stages: denial, anger, bargaining, depression, and acceptance. Each can be felt psychologically (or emotionally), physically, socially, or religiously. One doesn't have to experience each stage sequentially, and the time it takes to go from stage to stage can vary. In my case, I became stuck in the depression stage for a very long time. In the beginning, my grief was very messy. Have you ever bitten into a bright red, perfect apple only to find it dry, tasteless, and mealy? I'd have my hair done, wear makeup, and dress well, but all the goodness had been sucked out of me; I was bone-dry—a shell.

I thought I could get through my grief on my own. I

was wrong. I was broken. Keith graduated two weeks after Clinton died, and of course, we all attended the ceremony. Mom, Dad, and I were happy and proud of Keith's achievement. I recently looked back at the photographs of that day, and I see the smiles, but then I see the abject sadness behind our eyes. We were all wearing "happy" masks. After the graduation ceremony, with relaxation came more grief, more tears—I cried all night. How could people not see our pain? Of course, they witnessed it, but what could anyone say?

Three years later, I was still questioning when the nightmare would end and when I would begin to heal. How could I continue barely coping? I honestly thought that my grief and depression would never be over and I would never be happy again. Between 1997 and 1998, I searched for answers but didn't know where to look. In June 1997, we got a cute puppy—we called her Dutchess (Mom and Dad's dog was called Duke, and so she was our duchess, but we preferred our unique spelling of her name). I may not have realized it then, but she helped me with my grief.

When we went to buy her, I asked Mom, "How will I know which one to choose?" Like a Zen master, she replied softly, "The puppy will come to you." She was correct; there was no doubt that Dutchess chose me. There is something heartening about arriving home to a puppy wagging its tail.

With a new puppy in the house, the neighborhood children became frequent visitors, wanting to play with her. It was a welcome distraction. Dogs are amazing. After Clinton died, Mom and Dad sold his house, but Duke would still go and sit at his front door waiting for him to come home.

But then came all those events reminding us that our loved one was no longer with us. Clinton's birthday, Christmas, the anniversary of his death—and before all those was the first time we returned to our place in Whitefish. It was August 1997 when I walked into our condo and all the happy memories came flooding back. I walked into his room, and there on the chair were some new jeans he had bought and a pair of shoes. I could hear him saying, "I'll pick them up when we come back in the summer." Now it was me picking them up; grief overwhelmed me again. We had Dutchess with us, and I remember Mom and Dad hugging her constantly as if she were a substitute for Clinton.

We returned to Whitefish in December; it was the first Christmas without Clinton. He had loved the snow; winter was his favorite time of the year. We redecorated the condo, perhaps in an attempt to start again with new memories. Not trying to forget, but maybe move on. Dutchess loved the snow just as much as Clinton did, and I remember hoping that 1998 would be a better year for our family—it could hardly be worse. My memory of that trip was that an over-whelming sadness hung over everyone. Our grief was always in the background, lingering among our memories, material-izing at unexpected moments, and casting a shadow on any Christmas festivities we tried to engage in.

A New Life

Early in the New Year, I discovered I was pregnant. My parents were thrilled; a new family member, a new life, was just what they needed. Of course, the new baby would never replace Clinton, but a newborn was a sign of hope in bleak times. Garrett was born at noon on October 14, 1998. He had ten toes and ten fingers—he was perfect. We decided his middle name would be Clinton. My mother's bond with Garrett was immediate, and the joy and hope he gave her brought genuine, heartfelt smiles for the first time in so long. My labor lasted for two days, which I spent at home with Dutchie by my side. We gave her a receiving blanket so she would bond with the new arrival. It worked, and she loved Garrett!

I wish Clinton could have met Garrett; he loved chil-dren and would have been an awesome uncle. When news about the birth came, the phone never stopped ringing, and we received twenty bouquets. It was a true celebration of life—a new start.

I remember Dad telling me that we had a lot to be thankful for and so much to live for and that we had somehow made it through the most traumatic experience of our lives. However, Dad's business was struggling; the price of a barrel of oil had dropped by 80 percent. The effect this had on his customers was rolling over into his business. Keith and I were just starting our lives together, and we were also worried about the economy. Life has a way of balancing itself and is rarely without its struggles.

Christmas 1998 was very different from the previous year. Garrett brought hope and happiness; he was a shining beacon of light. I saw my mom and dad genuinely smile for the first time in a long time. My parents' love was intense, in a way that only grandparents who have recently lost a son would even begin to understand. Garrett was a special gift to a family distraught with grief. The extended family arrived and brought gifts for Garrett. He was a happy kid with chubby cheeks. I remember sitting, rocking him for hours and reading him books. I remember the pure joy he experienced playing in the bath. There was some of Clinton in him—he had the same personality. What a difference a year makes; we went from overwhelming, almost uncontrollable sadness to this bundle of superactive joy who gave us all something to look forward to. All of a sudden, life didn't seem as bleak. Perhaps everything was going to be okay.

Unfortunately, storm clouds were gathering on the horizon, and I was about to fall headlong into an abyss.

CHAPTER SIX

The Black Hole

Life is full of ups and downs for everybody, but for those who suffer from depression, the ups can be fleeting moments of relief in an unending, uphill battle to survive. Garrett's birth was a sign of hope, but it wasn't long before the weight of the feelings surrounding Clinton's death overwhelmed me once again.

As I mentioned earlier, I never read a eulogy for Clinton at his funeral. It was all too raw. I couldn't think of what to say; the words wouldn't come. I did write one later, but it took a lot of soul-searching; it was an incredibly tough exercise. I can't recall much of what I wrote, except I remember saying I was angry (a recurring theme for me) but at the same time proud that he had died helping someone, which was how he had lived.

I went to the accident site and read it aloud. It helped relieve my guilt about not delivering the eulogy at his service. I'm not sure what I hoped I would feel or how I thought it would help me, but it was something I needed to do; these were words that needed to be heard by the universe, sentiments that needed to be expressed. When I was finished, I folded the sheet of paper carefully and left the speech on the ground beside the railway tracks.

What I remember about that moment was that I felt incredibly hollow inside, empty, vacant, as if part of my existence had been stripped away. I suppose it had. Physically, I'd lost a lot of weight—I looked great. I'd bought new clothes and shoes, and my hair and makeup were perfect. The shell was solid, but it was just that: a shell. People, even my parents, never realized the chaos hidden behind my carefully constructed façade.

If I could go back and give some wisdom to my young self at that moment, I would say: *Journal your thoughts, talk to someone openly about how you feel, take control of what happens next, and do not suppress everything.* And finally: *You and only you control what happens every day.*

I missed my brother. I couldn't let go. How could I feel happiness and joy when my brother wasn't there to share my life with me or meet my kids? My depression was deep, dark, and unforgiving. I felt inadequate. I believed I was a terrible mother because I couldn't smile and be happy around my child. My new clothes were a charade, a way to bolster my self-confidence and give me power or control over my life. I felt that people didn't trust me—I didn't trust myself. I now realize that trust is the foundation of all relationships, and that's why, at the time, mine were all crumbling. For the most part, I simply wasn't present in my relationships.

Looking back, I should have focused on the things I was good at, not those with which I struggled. Confidence and trust are strengthened by continually learning and growing and by having sometimes difficult conversations with the people you love and care about. It's about always being authentic and truthful to yourself—being accountable. This is easier said than done, but you can start by questioning and shifting your perceptions about your world and life. Try sharing your vision of how you see things with others and be present—show up.

I knew I was in a dark place—the black hole, as I called it. I didn't know whether I could ever crawl out or whether there was life on the other side. I eventually talked to my parents and told them how hard life was without Clinton— as if they didn't already know. We all cried. Dad said, "We're all in this together; we'll get through it together." That helped, but . . .

The Sad House

Keith and I had only been married two years when Clinton died and had only moved into our new house the day before the accident. It instantly became a sad house. Our babysitter told me much later that the first time she visited our home, she felt an overwhelming sense of sadness and despair.

Grief hangs in the air like smog created by distant forest fires, slowly suffocating you even as you get used to its presence. It lingers and clings to everything, making it difficult to do everyday things such as laugh. We lived like that, in a haze, for years—a day-to-day nonexistence.

Marriage is tough in the best of times, especially during those early years when you are getting used to the other person always being there in your life. What I failed to realize fully was that Keith was also grieving. Clinton had been like a brother to him, and he took it hard. A newborn child should have brought joy, and Garrett did, but stress, responsibility, and guilt were constant shadows.

I built a wall around myself, hiding from friends, isolating myself, and creating distance so that it wouldn't hurt so much if I lost them. I just wanted to be alone or with my family—a close-knit circle sharing sadness, limiting my exposure to others. My friends, trying to help, would point out that I no longer laughed, and if they tried to talk to me, I just cried. Clinton's death consumed me.

My life was segmented; there were periods of real growth, and then there was faking it or hiding it until I made it through to the other side. However, I never could have answered the question: To the other side of what? Faking it meant caring for Garrett, organizing birthday parties, managing a dental practice, celebrating the birth of Keith's brother, Kirby, and his wife, Rachele's, daughter, and many other activities. Life doesn't stop, even if behind the façade of being "normal" you are, in fact, barely treading water. It took a lot of courage and energy to muster "happiness" around friends. It's hard to manufacture cheerfulness when another hidden dimension to your life constantly tries to intrude.

You need to ask yourself whether your coping mechanism is hurting or helping you. For my part, I felt that if I acted "happy," people wouldn't ask me how I was doing. Unfortunately, building walls around yourself is not a healthy way to deal with anything.

These were tough times, and I wasn't as present for Garrett or Keith as I should have been. I threw myself into my work and leaned heavily on babysitters and Garrett's grandmas. I loved my son to distraction. I'd hug him all the time, and we'd go to the park, and he'd have playdates. We'd visit Mom and Dad often, and when I was stressed, Mom would cook for me and even go and get my groceries. I'm not sure how I would have gotten through those days without her. At the time, however, I failed to consider that she was also grieving—yet another thing about which to feel guilty.

She wasn't the only one to look after Garrett; we were lucky to have extended family nearby. Keith's parents, Elaine and Al, are very hands-on as grandparents, and Kirby and Rachele lived only a few blocks away and would also help out with Garrett.

I was lonely in my grief. At the time, I believed I would simply get over my depression one day—it would magically end. I thought I could stick a Band-Aid on it by reading self-help books (rather than acting on their advice). Of course, I discovered that waiting it out was not a good plan. I was at a very low point; I felt like I was drowning and there was no life jacket. It wasn't until later that I learned, or maybe it was more that I accepted, that depression is a mental illness.

Grieving is a lot of work, both mentally and physically. Don't expect to be able to handle it all by yourself. Reach out to a counselor or other experts and get their perspective—see things through their eyes. Getting help was the best present I ever gave myself. Putting off getting help just prolongs the misery. If you are an analytical person, carry out a cost/benefit analysis. Heck, even if you aren't analytical, do one anyway!

Death Visits Again

Four years after Clinton's accident, the Grim Reaper visited again. That may sound dramatic, but I think it is entirely on point. It was June 2001; I was at home packing our trailer to go camping for the weekend when Keith called, totally distraught. He said, "Stacey, I just heard from a patient that Ryan was killed last night in a motorcycle accident." I couldn't believe it and kept saying, "No, no, no." It was happening all over again.

I had dated Ryan a few times before I met Keith. He was a close friend of Keith's and had been a groomsman at Kirby's wedding. We were all very close. We used to go on double dates with Ryan and his girlfriend. At the time of his death, Ryan was a newly minted firefighter. He had always lived life to the fullest. His mom always described him as a connector, a fixer; he planned events and got people together. Keith, Ryan, and another close friend, Kevin, often hung out together. They were the three musketeers; they'd travel down to Detroit Lakes and go to concerts. Ryan was a charmer with a ready grin and Kirk Douglas dimples. He was the first close friend to be taken from us, but he wouldn't be the last. Death seems to lurk in the shadows—so many souls have been taken before their time.

Ryan died a few days before I was the maid of honor at

my best friend Karyse's wedding. On the wedding day, wearing my bridesmaid dress, I had to go to the hospital to be treated for an asthma attack. It was not until decades later that I realized the asthma attack was almost certainly related to my high level of anxiety. Once again, I had to put on a brave face. I smiled for the wedding photographs and supported Karyse—the show had to go on, but Ryan's death brought Clinton's accident back into sharp focus with piercing pain. I spent the week cooking food for Ryan's parents—it's what we do. I also reviewed all my photographs and selected a bunch to give to his mom and dad. It was such a sad time; I sat and cried with his family. I also put them in touch with a Compassionate Friends grief support group. Joining a group like this that understands your grief can be incredibly helpful.

Keith and I were part of the funeral party, and I attended the viewing. I thought I had grieved enough over Clinton, but when I looked down at Ryan's face and saw the bruises, I could see Clinton's face. It all came back with unexpected suddenness—two young men had been ripped out of my life. So much lost potential. So much more baggage I would have to carry. Overlying the grief were fear and recognition of the fragility of life. *Am I next?* I may not have acted on it immediately, but at that moment, I understood the value of time and that it wasn't something to be wasted. This was yet another occasion where I should have realized that I needed to seek help.

Five months later, another very close friend died by suicide. Keith and I were devastated. We attended the funeral in Minnesota, and it was the first time we'd flown since the 9/11 tragedy—stress upon stress. Keith had known this friend all his life, and I'd gone to university with him. He and I had spent many hours traveling back and forth between Minot and home, chatting. Too late, we realized how distant we'd become in recent years. Mental illness is a struggle we don't all manage to survive.

We Have a Daughter

Four and a half years after Garrett was born, we were blessed with Katie. I say *blessed* because I had initially decided I wouldn't try for another child; the depression accompanying Garrett's birth had been too much. I remember listing a few more excuses to my Auntie Bev on a visit to Whitefish. We were walking together and she said, "Stacey, you don't want Garrett to be an only child, do you?" As silly as it seems, I hadn't thought of it like that before. I didn't realize I was already pregnant; Katie entered our lives only eight months later.

I had struggled with severe depression and anxiety for more than four years and had neither sought nor received professional help. The result was that I had made little to no progress in easing my mental strife. It was a big deal to get pregnant again, knowing that there was a good chance the pregnancy would exacerbate my depression considerably. I should have taken stock of my situation and found help earlier.

It is never too early or too late to go and talk to someone about your feelings. Unfortunately, I decided I needed to face my demons head-on by myself, live my life to the fullest, and not simply coast along avoiding challenges.

Avoiding looking for help simply escalates the situation. It never solves anything. It's easy to be so scared that you are a "damaged" person and so afraid that people will think you are "crazy" that you turn inward and do nothing. But ask yourself whether you honestly believe that's what people will think. Does that really make sense? I spent too long beating myself up before realizing that seeking help was a gift I was giving myself to ensure I would reach my potential.

As the weeks passed, I was positive I would have a boy. I felt so ill during the pregnancy that I couldn't even visit Mom and Dad because of severe nausea. I got colds, contracted bronchitis, and had asthma attacks. At six months, I went to my local doctor and asked for antibiotics for a nasty chest cold, and she refused. I traveled to Minot and the American doctor nearly hospitalized me immediately. That's when I decided to have Katie in the United States.

Katie was born on April 18, 2003. After the birth, my American doctor advised me against having more children. He said it was too hard on my physical and mental health. Sometimes you have to listen to the experts.

Back home, things didn't go as smoothly as I had hoped. I had retained a babysitter so that I could go back to work once Katie was about six months old, or at least fill in when needed. There was never any question that I would return to work after having Katie—why wouldn't I? That was the plan, anyway. In practice, I'd get into the shower and cry and cry. I just couldn't face going to work. I remember calling Keith one day to say I wouldn't make it in; he asked me why I was so sad. I had no answer; I simply couldn't stop crying. It wasn't long before that question was answered. It was too much—an energetic baby, Garrett, our business, housework, Keith, and the ever-present, lingering grief. I wasn't sleeping. Underlying anxiety kept me company throughout the dark hours. One evening, everything came to a head. It all boiled over; I was overwhelmed. I broke down, physically and mentally—my essence had been drained, and nothing was left.

I was an utter mess. I had to be honest with Keith and tell him it was unrealistic to think I could return to work full-time. I needed some time off work to focus on the children, myself, and my sanity. I also didn't want to miss out on watching them grow up. Children are young for such a short time, and I needed to be there and witness them becoming their own people. Keith agreed. I called the person who had been my maternity hire, and she agreed to return. I was thrilled and relieved; I could finally breathe again.

The best thing I did was ask myself, *What is realistic for me right now?* Ask yourself, What can you handle right now? Would part-time work, for instance, work better for you, or do you feel you need time to recuperate? Whatever the case, the key is to make a plan to find help.

Dr. Deb Is a Lifesaver

Six months after Katie was born, I was watching television while doing the dishes after supper, crying uncontrollably. A rerun of Larry King's interview with Patty Duke in 1999 came on. She was talking about depression. Patty suffered from bipolar disorder and said a doctor would tell you to seek specialist help if you had cancer, so why would mental health be any different? She talked about constantly crying, being angry, and being unhappy. Patty said her behavior toward people had been "hideous" and she had been in so much pain. She said she had received the correct diagnosis and treatment and wanted to share with the audience that there was a way forward.

It was an aha moment; it helped me emotionally destigmatize my condition. It was 2003, Facebook was several months away from launching, and it would be another five years before we would all be googling information. However, I researched postpartum depression online and decided to call my doctor in Minot. I had suffered depression after Garrett was born, but nothing like what I experienced after I gave birth to Katie. I hit rock bottom—and hard.

The doctor listened as it all came tumbling out: "I don't know where to turn; my life is in a shambles; I'm depressed; I want to cry all the time; I can't bring myself to be happy even for the kids, or anyone else for that matter."

He told me that I did have postpartum depression. It was a relief to know what I was dealing with. I knew I had to get better for the sake of my marriage, my children, my parents, and the rest of my family. Although I had always had an underlying level of anxiety and depression, I wanted to enjoy life as I had when Clinton was alive. I needed to learn to laugh again. I hated the fact that laughter had become a trigger for missing Clinton. I'd laugh and immediately wish Clinton were with me; I just couldn't let go of the fact that he was never coming back, that I would never see him again.

Remember, laughter is a natural stress reliever. We need it in our lives to achieve a state of balance. The person you are mourning would want you to laugh and start living again. It took me a while to accept this, but take it from someone racked with guilt every time she had fun.

Laughter is truly the best medicine. Consider calling someone right now who you know will make you smile or laugh out loud.

My doctor prescribed Wellbutrin, an antidepressant, and recommended I see Dr. Deb Johnson, a psychologist. Up until that point, I had refused medication. I'd thought I was strong enough to fight it myself. Now, I began to accept that things would not change until I became proactive. I accepted that this was how I'd been wired from birth; it wouldn't magically change overnight.

The Wellbutrin helped for a while. I should note that I have become an advocate for taking medication for depression, but only if prescribed by a doctor specializing in psychiatry. Much depends on whether you have a chemical imbalance. I was often told that if it works, continue with it, but always in combination with therapy. In my case, I add a third element: life coaching. Today, I only take anxiety medication and sleeping pills; they help me function. But I am not sure where I would be today if I hadn't used antidepressants when

I needed them most. At the end of the day, listen to a doctor you trust. If you don't trust your doctor, seek out someone you feel more comfortable with. And, even if you do trust them, get a second opinion. Never take your health for granted.

Dr. Deb was wonderfully patient and kind. After hearing about Clinton's accident, my sadness, and my anger, her first prescription was a book: *The Dance of Anger: A Woman's Guide to Changing the Patterns of Intimate Relationships* by Harriet Lerner. The book helped me identify where my anger was coming from and use it as a powerful medium to effect lasting change. It was one of the first books of its kind that I read; it made me confront my feelings. I began to ask myself what it was about my situation that made me so angry. I looked deeper at the underlying issues. I analyzed how I felt and what I felt. It challenged me to ask myself who was in charge of my feelings. It also allowed me to gain perspective and attempt, maybe for the first time, to see what I wanted to stand up for and what I was willing to let go of.

Looking back, I realize that I chose to stand up for myself. I searched for ways to deal with my problems and take on the responsibility of building a better life. I realized that I avoided conflict by cutting people out of my life, which was unhealthy. Once I began to deal with all of the relationships in my life, I let go of the feelings of hurt, pain, and anger.

Taking a proactive approach to our mistakes and challenges turns them into learning opportunities. *How could I have handled the situation differently? Could I have been more proactive and less reactive?* Remember, drama does not help in difficult circumstances; it can cause hurt and pain. Once you acknowledge a mistake, apologize, and learn from it, it loses its power over you. The other key to personal growth is not to dwell on the past—never add fuel to the fire. Learn and move on.

Writing my reactive thoughts, those that simmer beneath the surface, in a journal and then reading them out loud felt like releasing a balloon and watching those feelings float away. I would then write about how I might have handled things differently in order to avoid repeating the same mistake. The biggest thing I learned was to think before you speak, because you can't take words back. My mantra became: *Is what I am about to say true, helpful, insightful, inspiring, necessary, and kind?*

I recognized that anger was an honest emotion, but I needed to identify how much time I spent—or, more to the point, wasted—on being angry. I also needed to study its intensity. One's anger can be communicated in many ways and viewed by those around us differently. My relationship with Keith was in a deep hole, and it took several years to climb out of it. A key element when working through anger is to talk about it in the first person, as something you feel, rather than as an abstract thing that infiltrates your every word and action. I learned that the key was *to own my anger,* not to use it as a weapon to discharge my feelings onto others or just to make me briefly feel better.

I saw Dr. Deb once a week for an entire year. She helped me accept that grief lasts a lifetime, that it isn't something that magically ends one day. More importantly, she showed me that I didn't need to be sad all the time, that it was okay to enjoy life. Those sessions were the first time I could cry just for myself, not because of what I was trying to do for others or what they were doing to me. Dr. Deb introduced me to *the drama triangle.*

A drama triangle records and tracks what happens in an intense relationship prone to drama. It helps you see connections between one's personal responsibility and power, the potential for destructive behavior, and the way the roles people adopt can constantly change. Imagine the three points of an inverted triangle showing people's roles: persecutor, rescuer, and victim. These are the three facets of a drama. Drama has energy, which attracts or draws participants into conflict and then muddies the water so people can no longer recognize the real issues.

In the drama triangle, nothing is what it seems; victims

may not be genuine victims but rather people who feel they are being victimized or are at least acting that way. Victims feel browbeaten, hopeless, defenseless, and embarrassed, and they have difficulty making decisions and dealing with challenges. They lack joy and are unable to see a way through their plight. In my case, I felt I was the victim; my default standpoint was "Woe is me."

Persecutors are those people in our lives who tell us that it's all our fault. In a cruel twist of fate, victims often seek out persecutors because they feel guilty. Even when rescuers turn up, they are likely to perpetuate how victims feel about themselves because it allows them to remain dependent. It even allows them the opportunity to fail—to be rescued. Rescuers, by their nature, feel a need to help and are rewarded by diverting their focus away from their own insecurity and anxieties. In their own way, they are victims too. In this way, codependency between victim and rescuer can result.

The drama triangle can't exist without two players: the victim and the persecutor. It is they who instigate the entrance of a rescuer. The drama comes into the equation when people change roles. For instance, victims can reject rescuers; rescuers can become persecutors. As in a play, there can be multiple acts and multiple scenes. Persecutors try to control the situation; they bully and exhibit anger. They accuse the victim, condemn them, and dominate them. All participants, however, act out of self-interest. If one removes their ability to fulfill their needs, the triangle collapses. (For those who want to explore this further, I recommend *A Game Free Life: The Definitive Book on the Drama Triangle and Compassion Triangle* by Stephen B. Karpman, MD.)

Marriage Woes

Seeing Rhonda Britten on the TV show *Starting Over* was another turning point in my life. *Starting Over* was a reality show featuring six women who lived in a house together. They were all going through difficult times and getting help from life coaches, including Rhonda. Rhonda later founded the Fearless Living Institute. I related to her because she had gone through some incredibly challenging times—including, at the age of fourteen, witnessing her father murder her mother. Of course, the effect this had on her was awful, and she subsequently tried to commit suicide three times. Her final attempt was when she was twenty-eight; however, by the time she was thirty-four, she had completely turned her life around. Her story gave me hope.

During this period, my marriage was suffering. While I was focused on being the victim, I failed to recognize Keith's anger. He had lost his dearly beloved brother-in-law and two close friends in a matter of a few years. His anger was primarily directed at me, and my rage was focused on him. We fought—a lot. When frustration overwhelms us, we lash out, and those closest to us are often directly in the line of fire.

I lashed out a lot and immediately regretted what I had said. Today, when we are arguing, I give myself a time-out; I either ask whether we can revisit the issue later or, if I feel I am not going to be able to control my feelings, I leave the room. It's essential to understand who and what triggers you to want to lash out. Even if it is only for a few seconds, a time-out can give you a chance to ask yourself whether, in this case, silence might serve you better. Or whether you should take the opportunity to run through the pros and cons of saying something hurtful and escalating the situation. Take a second and ask yourself, "Is it worth it?" Feelings can build and fester, so getting them out in the open is crucial. Finding a close friend to whom you can occasionally vent is priceless.

Much later, I learned that shutting out those you love so you can wallow in your own grief just makes that black hole darker and more profound. Over the next few years, things got a lot worse for me because of this.

Dr. Deb told me that I was responsible for my own recovery and that Keith was in charge of his. Unfortunately, I couldn't feel Keith's pain nor understand what he was going through. I lacked compassion in his time of need. It's awful to say, but I don't think I cared about his grief. I was totally absorbed in my own recovery. Many times, I considered leaving him, even though none of it was his fault. I felt a strong need to escape the conflict.

Therapy helped me come to terms with the fact that I was still grieving the loss of my life with Clinton. I slowly realized that I needed to appreciate the life I had, not dwell on the life I once had. I had mourned what I thought had been a perfect life for too long. For too long, I'd blamed Clinton for taking that life away because he decided to drive on a foggy night when he should have known better. For too long, I'd blamed Marsha for calling him. I'd even blamed the universe. There was seldom cell signal in the area where Marsha stopped to call Clinton. But on that night, at that time, the universe decided that her call would go through. My anger was as illogical as it was destructive. But I finally knew I needed to move on to the next stage of my life. I was getting better; I would get better. I had a long way to go, but it was a start.

It was tough, but I became stronger. I went back to work after Katie's first birthday. Friends and acquaintances began noticing a change in me. I remember Marylou, a friend who also cleaned our offices, saying, "Stacey, you seem different;

what are you doing?" I told her about Dr. Deb and the difference she was making. Marylou began traveling with me to Minot every week, and we'd stop for lunch and talk. She was my mom's age. She always called Keith "her boy" because she didn't have children. She was diagnosed with the same type of cancer my mom contracted sometime later. Once again, I learned we should cherish every day as if it were our last.

Climbing Out of Depression

As I began to feel a little better, I began to exercise. I love being outdoors in nature, and I'd hike for miles. I find the smell of fresh rain therapeutic. Keith and I started entertaining at home. I cooked meals and baked fresh bread every week. We'd go camping; we boated; we went tubing; we played with Dutchie, our golden retriever; and I spent hours doing craft projects with the children.

It was around this time that I revisited my faith. When I was young, I always went to church with my grandparents, but I was usually bored and paid little attention. However, I wanted my kids to believe in God and embrace faith. To this end, I attended several churches and discovered many friendly and supportive people. After a month or two, I connected strongly with one couple, a pastor and his wife. They were patients at our clinic, and we began socializing with them and attending their church. I started meeting every Thursday with a circle of ladies at the church called the Alpha group. They helped me learn about the church and myself—we talked about challenges and triumphs. I remember feeling unconditional support and crying and laughing in equal parts.

Embracing my faith helped me, but another way to promote healing is to connect with your deceased loved one by doing something they loved to do when they were alive. Later, after my mom died, I decided that since she was a great cook, when I was missing her, I would dig out one of her favorite cookbooks and cook a recipe from it for dinner. Or I would go to a place we often visited together. It brought me closer to her, as if we were briefly together again, occupying the same space. Visiting family and discussing your loved one is another excellent way to keep them close. Remember, you may have to make the first move. Don't assume they will come to you; people lead busy lives. They can't read your mind, but you will be surprised by how willing people are to support you if you reach out.

This period heralded the beginning of my climb out of depression—or at least this particular period of this awful disease. I began to open up. The walls I had built started to come down, and I let people in for the first time since Clinton died. I volunteered to teach Sunday school. Garrett was in my class while Katie was in the church's nursery. Connecting with those children brought joy and happiness to me. They had such a willingness to learn. Remembering her childhood, Katie said to me recently, "Mom, I loved how you would allow us the freedom to paint, read, or just play. You never worried about the mess; you allowed me to access my creativity." I am so pleased I allowed Katie to explore her creative side.

It's easy when casting your mind back and remembering the tough times to forget the good things that happened— especially the everyday, simple things that make life worthwhile despite everything. As I mentioned previously, when Garrett was born, my parents were ecstatic. He had a familial resemblance to their son—my brother—and more than a dash of his personality. Dad would take his grandson to work with him on the farm. I treasure a photograph of Garrett sitting on the grain truck with his grandpa. Mom would take him to work with her at the office; he was her little sidekick, just as Clinton had been. They were integral to his upbringing and later to Katie's, not just weekend visitors. Garrett and Katie had their own bedrooms at Grandpa and Grandma's house.

As Katie got a little older, she loved cooking with Grandma. Mom was always at her happiest when she was baking or playing with makeup with her granddaughter.

Mom and Dad treated our kids like their own children rather than grandkids. To this day, Garrett and Katie talk about their grandparents, their influence on their values, and how they helped shape the adults they are today.

Mom called me every day at 7:00 a.m. to see how I was doing; she was a constant positive influence on me. I'd always ask her for recipes and catch up on family news and local gossip. We were as close as any family could be, a whole family, complete—almost. We'd spend every weekend with them, and we'd vacation together. Mom had a playhouse built for the kids, and in the summer, they would have a large pool set up—Garrett and Katie had a wonderful childhood with their grandparents.

We spent every Christmas in Whitefish, Montana. Mom would decorate the condo, we'd have great food, and the kids would open their presents. It would have been perfect if only Clinton could have been there too. Mom would never let us drive to Montana in the winter. Instead, she would give Keith and me train tickets as one of our Christmas gifts. Family traditions were important to us; luckily, they didn't stop after Clinton died. We'd all go skiing. I'd partner with Dad, and Keith would ski by himself because he was a black-diamond skier. We'd spend as much time enjoying hot chocolate and hot toddies as we did skiing; Dad and I loved après-ski!

Garrett would attend ski school, and Katie would go to day care to give Mom a break. Mom didn't ski; she hated heights and almost fell off a ski lift once, but there were always things to keep her entertained in Whitefish.

CHAPTER SEVEN

Regaining a
Sense of Self

The black hole, my longtime funk, receded in the spring of 2005. Counseling with Dr. Deb, who I'd been seeing since January 2004, had helped, and in many ways, I began to feel more hopeful. But grief can be addictive. Once it's got a hold of you, it has you in its power for life. For now, though, I was climbing out of my depression. I was dealing with the controlling, viselike grip of my addiction to grief, and for the next few years, I gained back some control over my day-to-day existence.

For the most part, I felt human. People often say, with a critical look, that some people wallow in their grief; meanwhile, specialists are fond of saying there is no right or wrong way to grieve. Grief for me, however, was a crutch. As long as I was grieving, I could permit myself to behave poorly, abandon the responsibilities I didn't want to face, hit the snooze button on my life, and wait for a magic genie to appear and take me back in time. The grief felt good. There was a sense of security and familiarity to it, like catnip to a tabby.

Fearless Living

Earlier, I talked about seeing Rhonda Britten on television in her show *Starting Over* and how her own story, and those of the show's contestants, gave me hope. I subsequently read her book *Fearless Living,* and I realized that I was indeed living in fear. It also made me consider the possibility of becoming a life coach myself. I'd always been interested in psychology. I'd taken a counseling course some years previously when investigating a career as a speech therapist. Although I was out of my comfort zone and fighting self-esteem issues, I surprised myself and excelled at a simulated coaching session. After reading Rhonda's book, I applied for her training program. Fear was an everyday experience for our dental patients, and I thought attending the Fearless Living program would help me when dealing with them. And perhaps I could also have a second career helping others. Oh, and of course, I lived with perpetual fear myself—especially fear of failure.

Fearless Conversations

I traveled to Irvine, California, for the first workshop in

mid-May 2005. It was called Fearless Conversations, and it was the first time I had gone anywhere without my family; I was thirty-four. Ironically, fear was all around me, but mine was under control for a change. I was excited. My parents, on the other hand, were racked by catastrophic thinking. They were convinced I would get mugged at the airport, the airplane would crash, I would be enticed into a cult, or I simply would never return. In an unusual display of decisiveness, I ignored my family's protestations, drove to Minot International Airport, and flew to Orange County, where I landed safely at John Wayne Airport. In the terminal, a nine-foot-tall bronze statue of the man himself looked down on me benevolently. His characteristic swagger seemed to give me a silent vote of confidence.

At last, I was doing something for myself, by myself. Maybe I was no longer lost, and this was the beginning of a life-changing adventure. I remember that in the Fearless Living Institute's introductory questionnaire, one of the questions was, "Who in your life would you like to have a fearless conversation with?" My answer was, "My parents."

At the end of the two-day course, I discovered that if I allowed myself to be vulnerable, I could learn and grow and become a better, more well-rounded person. I also met Coach Rosie in person at the conference; she had facilitated my tele-coaching group session earlier in the year. She was in her forties, a runner, slim, athletic, always smiling, and energetic. I called her the Energizer Bunny.

One of the facilitators took us through an exercise; she asked us to name an area in our life that we wanted to change. We then had to think of five things we could do to help move us toward that new reality.

The five things didn't have to be difficult, just "stretches," things we may have avoided in the past. These stretches could be as simple, in my case, as spending five minutes on a treadmill at home or jogging around the block a few times. Anything that pushed me a little out of my comfort zone.

Following this, we had to list five risks we could take to move us toward our goal. These needed to be a little more out of our comfort zone, more daunting than a stretch. In my case, this was going to the gym where other people could watch me and see my out-of-shape body.

Finally, we had to come up with five "dies." These were scary things we could undertake that would move us forward but which we thought would "kill" us. One of my dies was to run or walk in a 10K event and complete the course.

For homework, we had to undertake one stretch a day until we felt we could take a risk; once we had taken a risk or two, we had to attempt a die.

I remember the sense of accomplishment I felt when I went for my first die, which was walking a half-marathon—I thought I might actually die!

Acknowledging that I needed help and attending that first conference felt like an enormous leap. Later, I wrote in my workshop summary, "When I did a die, I felt alive; it was lots of fun." We grow only when we force ourselves to do something way out of our comfort zone.

It felt like I was continually stretching, risking, and dying during this period. I did small things to begin with, like simply asking for help, for support. I opened up to friends and asked them what they liked about me so that I could see myself through their eyes. I asked for help with my finances and admitted I was in difficulty. Then I took my first risk and asked my team at our dental practice to participate in a "Fearbuster" group session. I decided to reapply to dental hygiene school—nothing would stop me this time, which of course was in itself a massive risk—I was exposing myself to failure big-time.

Later, the dies came thick and fast, as if they were a backed-up drain that had been waiting for a plumber. I needed to get my life organized to get back on track. I created a vision board, which helped me take the first step.

I had thought of myself as a train wreck, only to discover

that I actually had enough value and wisdom to start coaching other people. I was, at last, allowing myself to be vulnerable and accept feedback without letting it destroy my self-confidence. I developed talks, went out into the community to share my story, and joined a Business Network International (BNI) chapter. Shy little me stepped out of her comfort zone and "died."

Fearless Foundation Weekend

One of my discoveries was that the best way I learned and grew was through conferences. The energy of listening to live speakers and interacting with coaches and fellow participants opened up possibilities for change that I did not get from simply reading a book. Since the workshop in California was so groundbreaking for me, I decided I wanted more. I went to Colorado the following month and attended a Fearless Foundation weekend. The workshops were powerful, and I began to understand who I truly was—I cried the whole weekend. It was a breakthrough; I forgave my brother for dying and forgave myself for being unable to save his life. Layers of judgment, and expectations of how I thought my life should be, were peeled away like layers of an onion, a metaphor that works well considering the copious tears I shed!

Attending weekend workshops such as these can be

transformative. I wholeheartedly recommend taking time to build your self-awareness. In my case, I wrote myself a forgiveness letter, began to understand the role expectations played in my life, learned how to vent safely, and recognized that my excuses prevented me from living my dreams. In essence, I became aware of my core needs.

The weekend sessions allowed me to see that I was wearing my brother's death as a badge of honor or perhaps a get-out-of-jail-free card. It gave me an excuse for not pursuing my goals. I knew that I had to make myself accountable—to myself. If I couldn't do that, how could I help others?

I was introduced to Rhonda's "wheel of fear" and "wheel of freedom" as part of her Certified Fearless Living Coach (CFLC) coaching course. The wheel of fear is a tool that helps a person identify their fears, identify the origin of those fears, and begin to overcome them. Imagine on a clockface the nine, twelve, three, and six positions. At the nine o'clock position, there is an event that triggers you; you then move clockwise to a fear response, then negative feelings, and finally, at the six position, self-destructive behavior.

The wheel of freedom uses a similar diagram, but you start at the three o'clock position with essential nature and move counterclockwise to proactive behavior, wholeness, and, finally, self-affirming behavior.

I learned how my own wheel of fear worked and iden-
tified my core fear—the thing that acts as my trigger. What
was I most afraid of? Rejection. That, and failure—for me,
they were intertwined. I was always fearful of not being liked
for who I was. Fear is natural and necessary. It is nature's way
of protecting us, but it has no boundaries and plays tricks on
us. I felt imprisoned by fear; it prevented me from being the
person I wanted to be. Fear was physical; it was an asthma
attack, my heart racing, a tight chest, headaches, sweaty
palms—anxiety. As a result, I became invisible. I avoided the
feelings of rejection and failure. I isolated and withdrew. My
failure was palpable. But my courses and work with Rhonda's
team allowed me to trade fear for freedom. I became more
aware and lived more in the moment, in the here and now,
not in the past where so many demons lurked. Freedom
makes you more creative. I started to see people as innocent;
I stopped blaming others and instead looked for solutions to
challenges. I refused to take no for an answer, even if it was
me being negative. I realized and utilized my personal power,
which gave me confidence. It was an attitudinal shift where
anything and everything became possible.

I learned how to use—or a better word might be *acti-
vate*—my wheel of freedom. It would take a whole chapter
to explain this, and in fairness, you'd be far better off buying

Rhonda's books and hearing it from the author herself, but if your wheel of fear is activated, you need to learn to move your wheel of freedom and access your essential nature. In short, the wheel helps you discover the real you and understand yourself. Knowledge is power. Knowing you are entering a fear cycle is the key to allowing you to see your life differently. I quickly learned that I wanted to live in freedom and not fear. Moving from one wheel to the other rewires the brain; it's not easy, and it takes energy.

By the end of the weekend, I knew that the way to heal myself was to work on my accountability. And to do that, I needed to keep asking for help—no one can be fearless alone.

The Wheels Weekend

I attended the Wheels Weekend in Colorado that fall, which was terrific. Even though I had already been to several workshops, it was my first time meeting Rhonda. Introducing myself to her and telling her how Fearless Living had changed my life was another die.

The whole weekend built on the work I'd been doing on the wheels of fear and freedom that I had started three months earlier, and my self-confidence grew as the weekend progressed. Building off of my first die, I spoke to the group about my own experiences, my trigger (the symptoms of which were the feeling I wasn't being seen, deflecting attention, and being invisible), and my essential resourceful nature. A person's essential nature is like a pie, with each wedge part of what makes up the whole. The pie I came up with consisted of ten traits: authentic, creative, compassionate, accountable, loving, beautiful, courageous, focused, generous, and trusting. Of course, all wedges are works in progress. They are things to which you can aspire to create the essential "you."

Like the wheels, the concepts of *stretch, risk,* and *die* are at the heart of fearless living, and in my experience, the abundance of joy that comes from undertaking them is miraculous. It's all about setting an intention and following through on it, proactively living your essential creative nature—actually being it. Later that weekend, two people approached me and told me that what I had shared helped them. It was so affirming to know that what I had said had a positive effect on someone else.

Fearless Loving

I knew that I needed to work on myself before I could begin to help others, and so I made the journey back to Colorado in January 2006 and continued the Certified Fearless Living Coach program by attending a two-day Fearless Loving workshop. I had spent my whole life seeking love from other people instead of finding it within me. Now, I was exploring my love for myself; it felt like a huge risk. To love me for who I was. To accept me, for me. To show myself compassion and acknowledge that I am enough. Once you can achieve this, you begin to see the innocence in yourself and in other people. I realized it was easier and healthier to see the innocence in other people rather than to immediately default to being afraid and defensive.

Fearless Loving was initially scary, but it allowed me to delve deeply into my relationship with my husband, my marriage, love, sex, and all the other messy stuff we have to deal with. We did several exercises centered on relationships in Colorado's clear mountain air. I remember one called "How can I love you?" It made me realize that if I didn't express to my husband what I needed from him, how would he ever know? Too often, we are involved in unspoken contracts where silence is taken as acceptance.

Meanwhile, I had become addicted—that word again— to being right, especially about love and pretty much everything else in my marriage. Soon, I realized this was not serving me well and terminated all my "silent contracts"— those unspoken agreements you create in your mind and expect others to keep. I decided to embrace my vulnerability instead of being fearful of it. In the future, I would let love in and no longer fear that my loved one would leave me. I would also embrace romance and physical intimacy in my marriage. In the following months, Keith and I learned a lot about each other; we began to communicate our feelings, and a new romance bloomed.

Looking at my notes from that weekend, I came across something I wrote. It is indicative of the power of confronting one's fears: "Loss is the one way we are shaped into our greatness." Being able to write that was a huge step forward in coming to terms with my brother's death.

Pathway to Change (Irvine, California)

I explored my past excuses, failures, and regrets as I entered the second year of my life-coaching program. Failure, or at least the fear of it, was my core negative feeling, and it was still holding me back in my coaching, relationships, and dental hygiene studies.

I had to let go of my past failures so I could no longer use them as an excuse for not moving on with my life. In a group exercise, I wrote a letter to myself listing how I felt I had failed my brother and then ripped it up and put it into a small black bag. I wrote that I felt guilty about not saving his life and not being a better sister, and I expressed how much I missed him. I knew he would have ridiculed my shame and guilt and told me there was nothing I could have done. I could see his grin; it was superimposed on my soul. I had to move away from those dark, self-destructive feelings and move on with my life. He would have wanted that. I threw the bag onto the floor and angrily kicked it.

Surprisingly, a fellow participant slowly bent down, picked up the bag, and hugged it. Her name was Julie; she was a petite woman with light brown hair. She looked at me with such kindness; it was one of the most transformative moments of the entire course. I knew then that I needed to embrace my perceived failures, learn from them, and show myself more compassion. She passed the bag to me, and I held it as if my life depended on it. And, of course, it did.

I used to get angry with people I felt had wronged me, and I'd hold grudges for years. I held myself to the same standards and hung on to the guilt of my mistakes, never letting go. That's why I kicked the bag; I was kicking myself. To fall back on an old quote: "Holding a grudge is like drinking poison and hoping the other person will die." I was slowly learning that the past should never detrimentally affect one's future.

I had been purchasing items on my credit card that I could not afford for some time. Successful people seemed to have lots of material possessions, and so I felt I had to buy lots of stuff to be successful. When I thought about it, I blamed my parents for always giving me everything I wanted. How could it be my fault? I didn't want to admit that I was avoiding being accountable for my choices around money or, for that matter, my relationships. But the Pathway to Change program, which built on the general theme of Fearless Living, encouraged participants to look deeper into their psyche. The course allowed me to dispel many judgments I had made about myself. It allowed me to face reality and see the true me without fear. That new awareness was massive.

Accepting the fundamental truth it espoused, the black bag exercise allowed me to be honest about my personal and business expenses. I shake my head sometimes at what I used to do and the thoughts that would rent space in my head. The past has a way of immobilizing you, of keeping you stuck there. But I learned that memories are created in the present moment. That was life-changing.

The value of programs like these lies not just in what you learn academically or experientially but in the support you get from others going through similar struggles. We all learn different things at different times and at different speeds. I hoped that at some point I could help Julie, who had hugged my bagged-up "failures" during the group session, with one of her struggles.

Financial Freedom (Denver, Colorado)

The awareness I gained during the Pathway to Change program with Rhonda and my Fearless Living coach, Wendy, allowed me to recognize what a poor state my finances were in, and so I took a weekend course called Financial Freedom. We first learned to set an intention about our relationship with money. I discovered that I was using money to keep score; the more I had or could spend, the more successful I felt. I enjoyed shopping and the act of spending money.

We'd all been asked to bring along a twenty-dollar bill, and one of the facilitators, Richard, gathered all the bills and ripped them up. My jaw dropped open. *What the ... He just tore up my twenty!* At that moment, I realized that it had value and that I had been disrespecting my money. It was the first step in learning to invest in myself, not in material possessions. The facilitators helped us identify what we valued and also identify our priorities—in my case, serving people, parenting, and being with family. That's what counted, not how many pairs of shoes I had.

I learned that once you get into financial difficulty, you become entrenched, repeatedly making the same poor decisions. Credit cards have a habit of making money disappear from view as if it isn't real—until the monthly statement appears. One of the exercises was creating a budget. I'd never budgeted before; I'd just spent what I wanted. I believed there would be no consequences; there hadn't been for most of my life. I recognized what a privileged upbringing I'd had, where money was never a problem. I learned to ask myself, *Why am I spending this money?* I began to question my purchasing decisions, asking myself whether I truly needed the item or was buying it to make myself feel better, more successful, and happier. The more I bought, the more I needed to buy. Ultimately, the course helped me break the vicious circle of unnecessary spending.

Fearless Living Foundation Conference (Toronto)

I attended the Fearless Living Foundation conference in Toronto in November 2006. It was my first conference acting as a volunteer assistant coach rather than as a participant. I was well out of my comfort zone and made mistakes, but I was beginning to accept constructive criticism and learn from it rather than let it destroy my self-confidence. I learned a lot from the other coaches in attendance. One of them asked me a tricky question; she said, "When you make a mistake, what do you do? How do you react?" It was ironic because I had been telling myself that I had performed terribly and was questioning whether coaching was the right path for me. But

I knew it was my fear talking, and so I challenged myself to determine what was true and what was false. Neither Rhonda nor any of the other coaches were being critical of my work. I began recognizing that mistakes were just learning opportunities, and I stopped wallowing in my "stuff." The weekend in Toronto made me realize that we must show up, ask ourselves difficult questions, make mistakes, learn from them, and grow. If I wanted to help others unlock their potential through coaching, I had to learn how to unlock my own. At the conference, Coach Rosie took me to one side and told me how much I had grown since we had first met at the beginning of my Fearless Living journey; often, one has to hear it from someone else to recognize and accept it fully.

Fearless Living Coaching

As part of my training, I started coaching at the beginning of 2006; it has been the most rewarding work I have ever done. There is something special about supporting people who are attempting to change their lives for the better. My job was to listen, ask questions, and help others on that path—something I discovered I excelled at. You might ask, why did I start coaching when I was the one who needed help? It's a good question. The answer, however, is not straightforward. Going through therapy and being coached gave me insights into myself that I never could have dreamed of getting in any other way. Once I experienced the power of having someone simply listen to me, ask questions, and gently guide me toward a greater understanding of myself, I wanted to learn how to be that person for other people. Experiencing it firsthand, I believe, makes you a better coach.

I learned so much from my clients that year. Coaching is never a one-way interaction between client and coach; it is dynamic. Although the client is the one being helped, it is impossible for the coach not to be positively affected. I spent more than 125 hours coaching and leading Fearbuster groups. These were support groups of four to six people. I would encourage them to discuss their situations and consider how they might have done things differently. I learned how fear shows up in people's lives—in trying to be perfect, being unnaturally hard on oneself, taking criticism too much to heart, and in a myriad of other ways.

I had ten clients and worked with two groups, one of which was our team at the dental practice. Yet one client had a more meaningful impact on me than anyone else. I'll call her Jill. After just three weeks of coaching sessions, she confided that she had been sexually abused by her uncle when she was young. She told me that I was the first person she had ever spoken to about the event that had changed her life. That session was a turning point for me. I told myself when I started coaching that if I could help one person overcome a significant trauma in their life and come out of it stronger, I would have achieved my life's goal. I told Jill that the truth has a way of setting you free and that this was the first day of the rest of her life. She would, at last, be free of labels, judgments, expectations, and excuses to live the life she chose for herself.

Jill's growth during our sessions was astounding. Initially, she was very angry toward the person who had abused her and toward those who had let it happen. I told her that she needed to forgive herself, have compassion, and forgive the others involved. Once she let go of the secret, she would become unstuck, and she could move forward with her life.

I've been asked on several occasions why I love to coach. Rhonda says, "Support gives us the courage to have confidence in who we are faster than if we relied only on ourselves." Helping people find that confidence is one of the most rewarding things I've ever done.

Regina and Dental Hygiene

The Stacey I was before my brother died was beginning to emerge like a butterfly from its chrysalis. It was as if I were being reborn in some way. To underscore this, at a Fearless Living coaching retreat, in the spring of 2007, with forty-three other coaches in attendance, I received the Grace in Growth Award. It recognizes exceptional commitment, growth, and tenacity while fulfilling the requirements of the coaching program. It was the first award I had ever received; I was stunned. It was empowering to be acknowledged for all the hard work I had put into dealing with my own life and also into coaching. Perhaps I wasn't such a failure after all.

My application for dental hygiene school was accepted, and in May 2007, at age thirty-six, I bought a house in preparation for attending school full-time in Regina. It would be just the children and me living there. It was hard to be separated from Keith, but he had to remain in Estevan to run our dental practice. He was also exploring a new business venture in Calgary, which kept him busy. Thanks to the courses I'd been taking, including Pathway to Change, I was back on course financially. Handling the house purchase all by myself was the ultimate die. I chose the place myself, I got the mortgage, I negotiated the deal (a good one), and for the first time, I felt independent. It was easier to get a mortgage in those days, and the fact that Keith and I already owned a house helped.

Mom and Dad had been against me taking the Certified Fearless Living Coach classes, and they were now putting up a lot of resistance to me taking the kids two hours away to

Regina. Mom even went so far as to tell me that if I insisted on going, the children would stay with her. Garrett heard her and started crying. That brought the situation to a head. I told her she was out of order and that the children were going with me. It was a knee-jerk reaction on her behalf, generated by catastrophic thinking. So I decided we needed to have a "fearless conversation." She said, "I can't bear to lose another child; don't leave me." I assured her that I wouldn't leave her and that we would see each other on weekends and speak by phone daily. It ended up being the most powerful conversation I ever had with her, and by the end of it, I realized how far we had both come since Clinton's death. Fearless conversations are excellent when communication with a loved one or coworker falters.

A Cozy Foundation

The kids and I moved in that summer, and I started classes in September. The new me juggled school, coaching, and Garrett and Katie. Luckily, Keith was supportive; he recognized that I needed to do something for myself to prove I could be independent. It was a significant growth challenge.

I felt I needed to regain a sense of myself, to see myself as more than someone's wife, daughter, or mother. Of course, all of those are essential roles, but if you are not your own person first, how can you be all those other things—play those other roles—with any real sense of integrity? Buying the house was also a good financial choice—I saved a ton of money that would have otherwise been spent on rent and three years later, I sold the house for seventy-five thousand dollars more than I paid for it.

The house was a 1,200-square-foot 1960s rancher. The inside had been refurbished and updated with refinished hardwood floors, and it was in a good neighborhood. The woman I hired to help me move in and unpack called it cozy—in a good way. Our spare furniture from Estevan fit perfectly, and it felt like home. I loved that house, and so did the kids. We had wonderful, supportive neighbors who stopped by to welcome us to the street. I had told the children that going to Regina was an adventure, and that's precisely how it turned out in many ways. Garrett was nine and Katie five. I firmly believe that children thrive with change; it helps them grow.

Keith sometimes came to see the kids and me on the weekends, and we'd binge on family stuff. We went to the park, saw movies, played board games, and went out for supper—it was a period when, despite our physical distance, we could fully connect as a family. My parents would visit, and I was pleasantly surprised to learn my mom and dad liked the house and were proud of me for making it happen.

Garrett was in grade four, and Katie attended the Montessori program at Wilfred Hunt School, only five minutes from the house. It had an after-school program, which was perfect. Enrolling the kids in that school was one of my best decisions. It focused on a child's ability to absorb knowledge from their environment naturally and learn by trial and error, and it stimulated their curiosity and innate love for learning. It allowed them to be in an environment that encouraged them to learn, explore, and be themselves. There were no desks, for heaven's sake!

Both Garrett and Katie thrived while we were living in Regina. Garrett could feed his love of history and dinosaurs, and his passion for Lego; Katie, an old soul who loved to dress up in bright, colorful clothes and seemed like she belonged in the 1960s, was able to explore her creative side and discover her artistic self. The Montessori school and Wilfred Hunt School were keen to involve the whole family, and Keith and I attended many school events: farm days, parent evenings, and many other activities. On Remembrance Day, we watched Garrett present his diorama of Juno Beach, D-Day, June 6, 1944; he was dressed as a soldier and looked so proud.

I have happy memories of those few years. Garrett and Keith worked on other dioramas, one full of dinosaurs and one replicating a battle scene from a war. Garrett was obsessed with history and had an uncanny knack for remembering all the details of historical events, even at nine. My dad, who also loved history, would tease him by making mistakes with dates or facts. With a serious face, Garrett would say, "You've got it all wrong, Grandpa; that's not how it was."

Some of my dental classes were held online, flexibility that helped make the seemingly impossible task of running a home, looking after two boisterous children, going to school, and learning to become a life coach possible. It's incredible how you can make almost anything work if you put your mind to it. I remember taking the kids to Chuck E. Cheese, a cross between a pizza restaurant and a video arcade featuring hundreds of interactive games, including dancing, shooting, car racing, bowling, hockey, and foosball. The food wasn't great—except for the salad bar, which was my favorite—but we loved that place. I would buy timed tickets and let Garrett and Katie play to their heart's content while I read a book or studied. That's a parenting win-win.

When Keith couldn't make it to Regina on the weekends, we met at Mom and Dad's house or occasionally at Keith's parents' home. His weekends with us in Regina were a welcome getaway. Our house in Estevan was a little barren because we had repurposed some furniture for the new house. As I mentioned earlier, Mom and Dad's place was Garrett and

Katie's second home, and Keith also often spent time there while I was away.

When we returned home for the weekend, Mom cooked special meals she had seen on cooking shows. For the most part, they were incredible, but occasionally, everything would go wrong, and we'd all laugh our tails off. During those weekends, Katie would spend hours cooking with Grandma—they were inseparable.

It wasn't all perfect, though; I still suffered from feelings of failure. I was working through it for the most part, but as soon as it came time for hygiene school tests, that fear returned like a thunderclap. Things came to a head in December 2007; Katie had been up ill all night, and Keith's mom drove the two hours from Estevan to look after her while I took my first important practical exam at hygiene school. When I arrived at the school, my head was throbbing, and the voices in my head—the ones that always told me I was a failure who would never be good enough—were going gangbusters. The voices won. I didn't just answer a few questions incorrectly; I used the wrong end of an instrument. Luckily, at the time I was working on Dexter, a realistic training dummy, scaling his lower teeth, but it was still an immediate fail.

The fallout was that I was required to retake that year's course. Ultimately, it was a blessing in disguise, but copious tears were shed. Yet so often, these things happen for a reason. I was able to spend more time with Garrett and Katie, and I began volunteering at their school. During this period, I had a dental school mentor, Elaine; she helped me realize this was the universe telling me to take a step back, regroup, and return stronger. I did just that. I found myself a rhythm and a routine. I remember her saying, "You are the CEO of your own life."

CHAPTER EIGHT

Death Comes Knocking—Again

While I was in Regina, Mom and Dad decided to build a new house at the lake. The "lake" was the Boundary Dam Reservoir—the head of which is about three and a half miles south of Estevan. The reservoir meanders some nine miles further south until it becomes Long Creek, which descends into the US west of the Noonan–Estevan Highway Border Crossing on Highway 47 into North Dakota.

It's a pleasant eight-minute drive from Estevan, almost forty minutes from Lampman. We used to have a small, old cabin on the lake with a wood-burning stove. It was our summer house, but Dad decided we weren't using it enough and sold it when I went to university south of the border. When we were young, Clinton and I loved the lake. Dad must have dragged us thousands of miles around that lake, on inner tubes or on skis. Our extended family used to join us—these were such happy days. I remember the smell of the barbecue, wet dog, wet kids, and what I call "lake perfume"—a mix of grass, trees, water, freshly caught fish waiting to be cooked, burning firewood, and charcoal. There's nothing like it.

My parents bought a lot only three doors down from our old summer home. The lot already had a small cabin on it, which they tore down; they were starting over. At the time, they were living in Lampman and were looking for a project. Building a new home to which they could retire seemed like a good idea, and they had always loved the lake. Construction started in 2007, and the house was completed in 2009—Mom looked at a hundred house plans before deciding on one that met all her needs; even then, she had it altered. The decision to build their dream house was a bit of a breakthrough for my parents, Mom especially. She said she had done enough grieving over Clinton and that it was time to move on. The new house was a fresh start but in familiar surroundings, nurtured by family.

Summer at the Lake and Darkening Clouds

Unfortunately, tragedy was once again waiting in the wings, as is its way. A lot happened during the build period, most of which was heartbreaking.

None of us knew that a dark cloud was coming; those

halcyon early days were full of excitement, anticipation, and a whole lot of fun. Mom and Dad had purchased another lot across the road from the building site, and Dad ran power to it so we could park two RVs there. We spent as much time there during the summer of 2007 as possible. The following year, we spent all summer with Mom and Dad at the lake in the RVs or in Lampman—one happy family. It felt like it would go on forever.

My parents built the house into a small hillside over-looking the lake, and its layout reflected how we lived. The master bedroom was on the main floor, and downstairs there were three bedrooms, allowing Garrett and Katie to each have their own rooms at Grandma and Grandpa's whenever they stayed. Even though the garage was oversized, Dad never parked vehicles in it; he used the garage as an indoor/outdoor entertainment space when we had parties.

Mom loved to do laundry and cook, and the laundry room in the new house was huge and the kitchen was massive. Because I'm not known for keeping a kitchen tidy—Mom always called me a messy cook—she had another kitchen built downstairs for whenever we stayed, which was every weekend, and for when we entertained, which was often.

That summer was idyllic. We just hung out and enjoyed each other's company. Katie learned to water-ski. Garrett fished and went tubing with Grandpa—and Keith, when he could escape our dental practice. I had signed up to walk the Queen City Marathon in Regina and hiked the lake trails for practice.

At one point late in the summer, as the leaves on the trees threatened to turn ocher, Mom told me she wasn't feeling well and thought she had cancer. I remember brushing it off and telling her not to be silly—looking back, that must have been a big admission for her because, in hindsight, she had been in denial about being ill for quite some time. Later, we found bottles of Pepto-Bismol in her office, inside her bathroom medicine cabinet, on her bedside table, and even more in the RV. Unfortunately, the one most in denial was me: I didn't want to contemplate another loss in the family, so I initially dismissed her concerns.

Around this time, Mom lost her best friend, Margaret, so the fact that she appeared depressed was not much of a red flag. That Labor Day, Mom cooked a beautiful family meal; my aunt and uncle joined us from Edmonton, and my aunt was concerned that Mom didn't look well. I still thought it might be depression and gave Mom my counselor's name. I also told her she should see a doctor but knew she probably wouldn't.

She and Dad were preoccupied with finding furniture

and all the fittings they would need for the new house—they would often leave straight from work and head out shopping. On one occasion in late November, they headed to Brandon, Manitoba, to visit some big-city stores. On the way home, they stopped at a fast-food restaurant, and my mother violently threw up. Dad was shocked; Mom had never had a delicate stomach. He called me, and I decided to take control and booked her an appointment with my doctor. Between Labor Day and that shopping trip, Mom had dropped forty pounds. There was no longer any question that something was wrong. I went with her to see the doctor, and he found a lump on her stomach. Despite her protestations that she was fine, he ordered several blood tests and MRIs. We waited for the results.

Whitefish and Dark Days

It was nearing Christmas, and Mom was determined we'd still take our annual trip to Whitefish. As usual, we went by train because Mom hated us driving through the mountains, even though she and Dad always drove. The kids loved going by train—to them, it was an adventure.

Keith, me, and the kids drove to Williston, North Dakota, eighty miles south of the border. The Williston railroad station consists of a red-brick, single-story building dating back to 1910, and the town itself was founded as a tent colony in 1887. It's an authentic frontier town, initially farmed by Scandinavian and German immigrants, and it always marked the beginning of our Christmas vacation. We'd take the Empire Builder; all told, its route would traverse approximately 2,200 miles from Chicago to Seattle or Portland and take around forty-five hours to complete. Its first trip was in 1929, and at the time, it was the Great Northern Railway's flagship train. Amtrak has operated this fantastic service since taking over the intercity rail service in 1971. Our section of the journey took almost eleven hours, and Mom always ensured we had bedrooms on board—there's nothing quite like sleeping on a rocking train!

Mom had not been looking good in the days leading up to the trip, and by the time we arrived in Whitefish, we still hadn't gotten the test results back from Canada. On Christmas Eve, she turned to me and said she was in terrible pain; she was as pale as a ghost, and I told her she needed to go to the hospital immediately. Dad took her while Keith and I looked after the children. After what seemed like an eternity, Dad called and said I should get to the hospital immediately. They had run some tests and done a biopsy, and when I got there, the doctor informed us that Mom had cancer.

By now, you know I am very emotional, and so the

C-word hit me like a ton of bricks. My thoughts immediately leaped to the loss of Clinton; I didn't want to lose Mom too. I stayed with her that night, and she told me, between bouts of vomiting, that she didn't want to die and wanted to see her grandchildren grow up. But the following day, the news worsened. The doctors told us that she had stage four stomach cancer and that there was little they could do for her except keep her comfortable—a strange thing to say, "keeping someone comfortable," when that is precisely what is impossible.

The doctors meant, of course, that they would pump Mom full of drugs until she no longer felt anything. She was in agony. Dad and I stayed until they managed to get her pain under control. The entire experience was surreal—we were supposed to be opening presents, having Christmas dinner, not watching over someone dying. My mind flashed to Clinton's instantaneous, unexpected death, and I wondered what hell my mother would have to face over the following hours, days, or weeks. How long would she have to endure this? We didn't know. I thought of Katie and Garrett, envious of their ignorance of what was happening; they had no idea how sick Granny was—how could they? How was I going to tell them?

On the twenty-seventh, Mom was still in the hospital; I

stayed with her almost day and night. That evening Dad and I went to get supper, only to be interrupted by a call from the hospital. Mom had taken a turn for the worse, and they needed to operate—now! The tumor needed to be removed; she had sepsis, and a chain reaction was occurring throughout her body. By now, they knew that the cancer had spread; later, we were told it had almost certainly started as ovarian cancer. Dad gave the doctors permission to operate, despite Mom saying she did not want the surgery. She was in so much pain and on so many drugs she didn't know what she was saying.

We knew the surgery was just a stopgap, a delay, to give her enough time to die on her own terms, hopefully at home. After two and a half hours in surgery, she returned to her room—she had survived. I remember seeing her on a ventilator, hooked up to a cacophony-inducing assortment of machines. When she eventually woke up, she asked for a smoke. That was Mom.

I went down to the small chapel in the hospital to say a prayer. It was simple—I wanted my mother to get better. The news was so grim that I was having difficulty grasping reality. It couldn't be my mom; this was a mistake. After a few kind and comforting words, the pastor came over to me and hugged me; I cried but felt better. Walking back to Mom's room, I realized that I was coping much better than when

Clinton had died. This time I could and would ask for help. My experience of being coached and coaching others brought a paradigm shift in my thinking and coping mechanisms. I contacted the dean of my dental school about quitting the course to care for my mother. The dean was supportive of anything I wanted to do, but it was Elaine, my dental school tutor and mentor, who told me not to give up but just take some time off to deal with this family emergency.

My dad, however, wasn't coping well with Mom being so ill; he couldn't bear to see her like that. The one thing that helped him during stressful times was driving and looking after his business. He told me he had to go home to attend to his company; he left in a snowstorm and drove the six hundred miles to Lampman, trying to distance himself from the pain. The journey took him a little over eleven hours. What could I say? He called his brother, Gary, in Edmonton, and he and my Aunt Bev drove through another snowstorm to get to us and be with Mom. They were and are like my second parents. Their son Kirk, who was learning to fly, flew down for supper and then left—again, family is important. Then Dad's cousin Glen and his wife, Bev, came from Kenosee Lake. Bev, a nurse, was one of Mom's closest friends. It was a family joke that we had three Bev Grimes in the family, and two of the three were with us in Whitefish!

The clan gathered. After four days, Dad returned. Mom had stabilized and was gaining a little strength. She wanted to go home to Lampman.

Keith packed up the kids and headed to Regina, where he dropped them off with his parents before heading back to Estevan. Once there, he called Mom's doctor to let him know what had happened and to ask for help getting her home to Canada and into Regina General Hospital. By now, it was a week into the new year. Mom's doctors in Whitefish told us that we only had a short window of opportunity to get her home before she became too ill to be moved. We arranged an air ambulance, a Beechcraft King Air, and loaded Mom into the aircraft. The journey to Regina took two hours. Mom hated flying, but it was the only way—Amtrak, in this case, was a nonstarter.

The old voices in my head returned with a vengeance during the flight. The ones full of doom, gloom, and guilt, of things unsaid or said in frustration. I pleaded with God to give Mom another six months, maybe a year—I told him I couldn't lose her too. Lying on the medical sled, Mom looked frightened of flying, illness, and death. I held her hand. The drone of the turboprops failed to drown out the voices, the memories, Clinton, the inevitable loss of my rock—my mom.

Mom's "Condition"

When we landed at the hospital, my Aunt Judy met us, along with a Nurse Ratched, who ordered us to put on gowns and mask up because we were coming from another hospital. She quickly became a thorn in my side, and it wasn't long before we crossed swords. She complained about me not following all of her rules; I stood up to the battle-ax and said that, as these were Mom's last days, I didn't care for her regulations when they were detrimental to Mom's well-being. Nurse Ratched eventually backed down and left us alone. Mom's sisters and brothers visited, along with many friends, and she perked up a little, telling them that she had a "condition" rather than calling it that other C-word. It would be a little while before she fully came to terms with what it meant. I remained by her side constantly, but she often asked for Dad. He was fighting his own demons, though, and they were telling him to avoid this painful situation. Later, he told me he didn't want her to see him cry. They had been together since she was fifteen, and she was his rock too.

We all deal with our grief differently; sometimes, it's hard to understand how it affects others. Dad and I both felt varying degrees of guilt. Neither of us thought we had truly appreciated Mom and everything she had done for us over the years. She was always a silent hero, working in the background, unnoticed. Just because she didn't expect, or even want, accolades didn't mean we shouldn't have showered her with them. Guilt personified is when you take someone you love for granted. Dad was broken. He didn't know how to fix himself or his wife, so he retreated into his grief only to emerge into a world of guilt.

One night, after Mom had been in Regina General for two weeks, she pulled out her IV lines and told the nurses, "I want to get the fuck out of here." They did a CT of her brain the next day to ensure she was still lucid—a true story. But the cancer had not spread to her brain; like most people in these circumstances, she just wanted to spend the rest of her days at home.

Given her condition, I wasn't sure if this was a good idea. However, she threatened to take a bus home, so I talked to her cousin-in-law, Bev, who helped me make the arrangements. She was incredibly helpful; she'd had brain surgery some years before and could relate to what Mom was going through. We took clean clothes to the hospital and applied some makeup, then Dad came to pick her up and take her home to Lampman.

The following week was tough. I had planned to go home every weekend, but Garrett caught a bad cold, so I was stuck in Regina—I knew the last thing Mom needed was a cold on top of everything else. However, I had unreasonably demanded of myself that I be with my mom every minute of every day, which racked up my guilt levels to ultra-high. So instead, I called her three times a day and talked to Dad frequently. With the help of some home care nurses, he took fantastic care of her; he would massage her feet, which made her feel a little better. Occasionally, she'd rally a little and go to the office to help with the end-of-year financials. She was weak, but the family business was important to her, and she loved her job.

Once Garrett recovered, I went home—a few weeks before she passed. I told Mom I would take the kids out of school and look after her full-time, but she wouldn't hear of it. At this point, we were still living on hope—if not for recovery, then at least to slow the cancer and give her some more time. We made an appointment with the cancer clinic in Regina to try chemotherapy. Sadly, she died a week before her first session.

At the end of January, she insisted on making home-made fries and lobster even though she couldn't keep anything down herself. I always felt that cooking for her family was like a language of love for Mom. It was heartwarming but so sad at the same time.

Please Don't Do That;
I Am Not a Duck

A few days later, I had to return to Regina to handle a few things. I was only back in Regina a few days before I got a call from Dad's sister Barbara telling me to come home quickly; Mom was back in the hospital. I dropped the kids off with Keith's parents and drove straight to the hospital. It was the longest two-hour drive; all I could think of was that Mom would die before I arrived. When I finally got to the hospital, Dad looked dreadful, so I told him he needed to go home and rest. I called Keith and said to him that Mom didn't have long. A nurse came in and drew some blood; it was dark and thick. She looked at me, and her eyes told me it was nearly time.

I called Dad, and he headed straight back to the hospital. While we waited for him to arrive, Keith and I each held one of Mom's hands, and I stroked her hair. With a sincere look, she glanced up at us and said, "Stacey, please don't do that; I am not a duck." We burst out laughing—Mom could always make us laugh, even in the darkest moments. Then she closed her eyes and left us alone. It was Friday, February 13, 2009. I didn't just lose my mother; I lost a part of me.

Mom's older brother Darwin and his wife arrived just seconds after she passed. They were the same family members who had told me that Clinton had crashed his truck all those years ago; Mom was the first of her siblings to die, and this time it was I who had to tell them the news. Dad arrived ten minutes later. To this day, I believe she chose to die during the brief period he was absent—she knew what a difficult time he had handling death.

On the journey back to Lampman, Dad called my Uncle Gary to tell him that Mom had passed; I could see he was barely holding himself together. We are never ready to lose a loved one, no matter how much we tell ourselves, "They are in a better place." When we walked through the front door, the house was empty. It wasn't just the silence that hit us; all the energy had been sucked from it. That house was never the same again; it became a hollow shell.

Weeks passed, and I still didn't want to go back to school—when things got tough, my fallback was to quit. It was easier than dealing with my issues. A week or so later, Dad told me that he was returning to work and that I had to return to school. I wasn't ready, but I knew he was right.

Grief was my familiar and gruesome playmate; I drifted into depression despite the support I received from Wendy, my Certified Fearless Living coach, and Elaine, my dental hygiene mentor. As I've mentioned, Mom used to call every morning; it was our thing. For the longest time, each day at

7:00 a.m., I expected the phone to ring, and sometimes I even thought I heard it. How can silence be so deafening? Mom and I would often speak five or six times a day. How do you fill that big a hole in your heart, in your day, in your soul? I coped, barely. Routine was my crutch. I got up, looked after the kids, put on some makeup, and pretended everything was okay.

In March, Keith and I fulfilled my mother's final wishes and went shopping for white plates, silverware, and decorative items for the lake house. During those long vigils by her bedside, she had told me exactly how she wanted the house set up. Dad moved in shortly after Keith and I had followed Mom's instructions and staged the lake house as she had described. Over the following months, while I was in Regina at school, Keith had supper with Dad most evenings.

During this time, Dad and I would discuss our grief on the phone. He said he would grieve for a year and then be done. I tried to tell him it didn't work like that, but he said it would work for him. Our first summer without Mom was tough; Dad and I struggled in our different ways, as did Keith. Katie and Garrett missed Granny, and we often reminisced about her—I am not sure if it made things better or worse. In the meantime, I continued with school and knew I would see my degree through to the end. It was what Mom would have wanted.

Whitefish without Mom

In early fall, Dad said, "Let's go to Whitefish, Phoenix, and Las Vegas for Christmas." After a year of research, he had bought a new airplane, a Pilatus PC-12 NG. Although he loved to pilot himself, this airplane was too technologically advanced for him, so he hired a pilot to fly us out. I don't know how much of this was done to take his mind off losing Mom, but planning the trip gave us all a way to occupy ourselves. I was nearing the end of school, but I still had a week of seeing patients at our Estevan office before we set off on our vacation.

In Whitefish, we did the stuff we always did; we decorated the condo for Christmas and went to dinner with friends, especially old family friends like Kelly and Joanne. They had a place in Whitefish but lived across the road from us in Estevan; I've been friends with Joanne since ninth grade. We skied, cooked suppers together, and talked. It was all so strange without Mom, especially decorating for Christmas. During festive times like these, your soul misses your lost loved one's energy. They leave a void. Life went on but with less laughter, less love, less color. Mom had always been the glue that held our family together.

Dad wanted to give the pilot some hours on the new airplane, so we flew to Phoenix and rented a beautiful condo.

It was chilly, but the kids still managed to swim. It's funny how kids don't feel the cold as much as us "old" folks. We also shopped—a lot. I remember a store called Kiss Me Kate, a fantastic boutique—as soon as Katie saw it, she kissed me on the cheek. Some memories are of the simplest gestures, yet they mean so much. I cherish these small moments that are now frozen in time.

From Phoenix, we headed to Las Vegas, always a favorite destination for the family. We stayed at the M Resort on the South Las Vegas Strip, away from the main hustle and bustle. It was convenient because we'd flown into Henderson Airport, close to the hotel. We all felt depressed that Mom wasn't with us, and we were not ready for the full-fledged Vegas experience.

During the first few months of 2010, my relationship with my dad silently fell apart. There was no drama; we just didn't spend much time together. We had always lived connected lives, seeing each other every day, but the specter of death and the fog of grief were all too much. I missed Dad so much it hurt, but we both had to carve out new lives for ourselves without Mom. I'm not sure we knew how to do it together—so we did it apart. Mom and Dad were like Keith's and my best friends; we spent almost all our recreational time together, and when Mom died, there was a catastrophic change in the dynamic. On the face of it, Mom's death should have brought us closer, but it pulled us apart. The challenge was that we all grieve differently, and our methods are not always compatible.

In February, about a year after Mom's death, Dad told me he had met someone. I swear my heart stopped beating for a few seconds. Her name was Norma. She could have been the Queen of England, and I still wouldn't have been okay with her dating my dad. She was a widow, and Dad had been the best man at her wedding.

I felt abandoned, completely alone. I had never met this woman—she just appeared in my life. Negative and irrational but real feelings flooded my brain, attacking my psyche. *Dad doesn't love me anymore; he doesn't love our family; obviously, we aren't fun to be around anymore; he doesn't want to spend time with us; everything is being destroyed; it's all Clinton's and Mom's fault for dying.* Once again, my anger was misdirected.

As I said earlier, grief is personal; it's not one-size-fits-all. In dating Norma, my dad wasn't trying to erase the past. His coping mechanism was to get on with his life; he just needed to make the most of it and couldn't handle my grief in addition to his own. The reality is that Dad was always there for us, and he never stopped loving us. But at the time, I just couldn't accept that he had a "new" family.

He spent a lot of time with Norma's family, which exacerbated my hurt—and was an unintended slight. It was easier to turn away, to distance myself from Dad and his new relationship. He was happy with Norma and her family; he talked highly of them. I tried to be happy for him—I really did—but all that time I kept thinking, *I'm still grieving; why aren't you?* We sometimes spent time with Norma and her family, and they were friendly and welcoming, but I never felt like I belonged. He had two families now, and we were sometimes not his priority. Dad spent the second Mother's Day following Mom's death with Norma and his new family—and that hurt more than I can say. I confronted him, and he simply hadn't realized it would cause me so much pain. He never did it again. I wonder whether it was the personal slight that hurt me so much or seeing so clearly that he had moved on with his life.

Sometime later, I discovered that he always talked about Mom with Norma. In the act of telling my story, it's only now that I've come to fully understand the differences in how people grieve. I should have respected Dad's right to grieve in his own way; I was hard on him and had no right to be. I dwelled on the past, and my dad decided to focus on the present and build a future. Which was healthier?

From my skewed perspective, my life had been perfect

before Clinton and Mom died, and I was jealous of families who were still intact. Jealousy, however, is such an unattractive emotional response. I should have considered that Norma, too, had faced a great loss in her life.

The New Normal Creates New Traditions

At some point, I realized what a gift my family was, and my focus turned toward them. Instead of longing for what I didn't have, I preoccupied myself with what I did have and spent my days getting myself and the children reoriented to "normal" life. Keith's practice was doing well; I was, at last, a dental hygienist; Kate was seven and had a crazy zest for life; and twelve-year-old Garrett was successfully managing his ADHD.

I used to love watching Katie dance. There was a freedom to it that gave her such genuine pleasure. When she danced, I could see she was constrained by neither the past nor the future, and as I looked on, neither was I. We always had kids visiting the house; there were birthday parties and playdates, and I felt like I was getting back to my happy place. We vacationed in Hawaii, cruised the western Caribbean, and visited Castaway Cay, the Disney island. Life was good. I knew I would always grieve, but I recognized that the intensity of my grief lessened with time.

But in life, nothing is ever completely static. My ability to survive loss, grief, and depression was about to be tested again—and very soon.

CHAPTER NINE

Dad's Fight for Life

I n 2012, a global energy services and equipment company, Schlumberger Limited, approached Dad with an offer to buy his company. It was a big deal. Schlumberger, founded in 1926, operated in 120 countries at the time and had over 86,000 employees. They had been buying up pumping businesses in Western Canada, and here they were in Lampman (by the early 2000s the population had fallen to 675), wanting to purchase our family business. I'm not sure if Dad was flattered, but he wasn't sure he wanted to sell the company. Over the years, he sold over fourteen thousand of the unusual-looking, energy-efficient HG pumpjacks and had around 90 percent of the local market.

It was a big decision. I used to say that Dad had three children: Clinton, me, and his company. As I mentioned earlier, in our small corner of Saskatchewan, my dad was a big deal. Mom and Dad had worked in the business all their married life. He'd lost Mom; now he felt he was losing his business. He asked his brother, Gary, what he should do and consulted with some of his senior employees. Gary felt that Dad should begin to take things easy and that this was as good a time as any to sell the company.

However, Dad wasn't going to jump into anything, and it was not until March 10, 2014, that the parties ratified the sale. He displayed the highest level of integrity and ensured that his employees' jobs were secure before signing on the dotted line.

Life Turns on a Dime

The next day Dad went in for a bunch of blood tests. He hadn't been feeling well, and I suspected he had a kidney infection, so I'd made him a doctor's appointment and ensured he attended. I was sure it was just his kidneys, so I didn't go with him. Two days later, he returned for the results, and I went to have my hair done at a local salon. The doctor's receptionist called me at the hairdresser—we live in a small town—and told me I had better come to the office. She confided that Dad had received some bad news. My heart dropped through my stomach. I felt sick; it was the same feeling you get when you are in a car accident, an immediate gut punch that makes you want to throw up.

It turned out that he had an enlarged prostate—so enlarged that he wasn't emptying his bladder sufficiently, which was detrimentally affecting his kidneys. His blood test results were scary. I stared at the numbers for a while, not believing them—they could not be accurate. A normal prostate-specific antigen (PSA) level is less than four; Dad's was 747—just like the jumbo jet. His glomerular filtration rate (GFR) was four; a normal GFR should be sixty or higher (below fifteen, and your kidneys are likely failing). It was all too much to absorb.

Things were so bad that the doctor said he would call an air ambulance to transport my father to the hospital in Regina. True to form, my father would have none of it; he said he was okay to drive himself. I'm not sure what the doctor would have said if he had known that my dad would take a detour to visit his office to sign some checks before making his way to the emergency department. Nothing I could say would deter him, so I packed a bag for him and one for me. I called Keith and told him the news. When I mentioned the lab results, he said, "Oh my God!"

After signing the checks, Dad drove us to Regina as if we were just going shopping. When we arrived, the kidney specialist said, "Mr. Grimes, I've been waiting for you. I expected you some time ago; this is an emergency." Dad was still in denial and said, "Don't worry about me; see to some of these people in the waiting room. I'll wait." The doctor took his arm and said, "Mr. Grimes, you are the sickest person here."

Life can be cruel. Dad had only sold his business four days earlier and was planning his retirement. His initial diagnosis was acute renal failure due to obstructive uropathy, but we all knew something worse was hiding in the wings. I stayed with Dad's sister Auntie Judy in Regina; she tried to reassure Dad that everything would be okay. People do that, of course, but even though she had survived many health problems, I knew the words were paper-thin. This crisis wasn't something Dad could simply shrug off, not this time.

A few weeks later, after an MRI, blood tests, a prostate biopsy, and generally being pushed, pulled, and prodded, Dad was diagnosed with stage four inoperable prostate cancer. Two Gleason grades are attributed to biopsy samples; the scores are based on a distinctive pattern the cells exhibit as they change from normal to cancerous cells. A pathologist looks at the primary and secondary patterns in the cells and attributes them a Gleason score, the highest being ten. In Dad's case, his grades were four plus five, for a score of nine; a score of five means that the cells have mutated to such a degree that they are almost unrecognizable as normal cells. Dad's cancer put him in the highest-risk group. The news was dire and getting worse; the cancer had metastasized and was in bones. The doctor gave him four months to live and advised him to get his affairs in order. For the first time, reality hit him, and he cried. He said the same thing my mother had said: "I want to see my grandchildren grow up." I had to leave. Alone in a hospital bathroom, I cried and cried massive, earth-shattering sobs. *Not again, not again.*

I can't live in a world without hope, so I told Dad, "We can fight this together; there is always hope." I wasn't sure we could win, but I knew we'd give the disease a run for its money. Dad looked at me and said, "Hey, Stacey, I'm going to beat this."

In those early days, I relied on Keith's medical knowledge to help me decipher all the medical jargon; before going to dental school, he'd earned a double major in biochemistry and anatomy. It was tough for him because he was close to his father-in-law in a way few sons-in-law are. He researched and gathered information on people who had successfully fought prostate cancer. Flipping through the thirty-page medical report, Dad felt a glimmer of hope. Looking at him, I hoped he would have enough energy and determination for the fight of his life.

Keith told Garrett and Katie that Granddad was in the hospital. We decided they deserved to know the truth and told them their granddad was ill. Although Katie was too young to understand what it meant, they both cried. Garrett was a sensitive child, and it hit him hard. Much to my father's annoyance, I called his brothers and sisters. He thought I shouldn't have bothered them.

Dr. Google became part of my life. What I discovered was depressing; the life expectancy of people with stage four prostate cancer is not good. The five-year survival rate drops to 30 percent when it spreads to the bones, other organs, and lymph nodes.

In those early days, I struggled to balance my father's wishes with my desire to do anything to help him survive. He told me that he wasn't sure whether he wanted to undergo chemotherapy; his business associates in China had been talking to him about herbal medicine. I sat down with him and told him I wanted him to live and that the only way I knew how to do that was to get him the best possible care.

We were, of course, in a privileged position. Dad had worked hard and run a successful business since his twenties, which he had just sold. Our dental business was going well. We would not let paying for medical care in America stop us from getting Dad the best possible care. We'd mortgage our houses, the business, and anything else if need be.

The Fight Begins

My anxiety was off the charts. Keith came to my rescue, said we needed a second opinion, and suggested the Mayo Clinic. His advice gave me something to do, and I called them immediately and got Dad an appointment. On April 4, 2014, Dad and I left for Rochester, Minnesota; Keith followed in a few days. Dad was so weak we had to transport him everywhere by wheelchair; luckily, he still had his airplane, so we could fly to Minnesota with the minimum amount of fuss. I was familiar with the clinic, as I had been a patient there and I'd been impressed with the care I had received. Later, Keith confided that Dad had looked so bad as the airplane door had closed that he had doubts he would ever see him again.

At the Mayo Clinic, the tests were easy; the challenging part was meeting with doctor after doctor and never getting a direct answer. Every time, Dad would ask, "How long do I have left to live?" Most of them said about six months. However, a young, down-to-earth intern whom Dad especially liked broke ranks. He said, "Mr. Grimes, I do not have an answer for you; I am not God. You may have two months, two years, ten years, or even twenty years. Just live day by day and be content that you are here today." This mindfulness approach of living in the moment resonated with us, and Dad thanked the doctor for giving him hope. There was a noticeable difference in approach between the Mayo Clinic and the many doctors we spoke to in Saskatchewan.

The Mayo Clinic doctors diplomatically suggested that Dad and I stop using Dr. Google. Dad said, "Stacey, none of us are good at everything; pick the stuff you are good at and choose the right experts to join your team." Just as I started to spiral into "woe is me" territory, an executive at Schlumberger contacted me. They had heard that Dad was seriously ill, and they introduced me to a company called Private Health Management. The company helps people facing severe medical issues manage the healthcare system. I googled the chairman, Leslie Michelson, and discovered that he had been the former vice chairman and CEO of the Prostate Cancer Foundation. I also found an article he had written a few years earlier titled "What Steve Jobs' Death Teaches Us All About Our Own Health Care."[1] I emailed him and got a telephone appointment with the man himself. It's surprising how far you can get with determination and, of course, desperation.

Before the call, I sent him all of Dad's test results and related information. Dad couldn't face the meeting, so I handled it alone. Michelson told me that he had reviewed the file and explained that Dad would be in for the fight of his life. However, he knew of several treatment options that

1 Leslie Michelson, "What Steve Jobs' Death Teaches Us All About Our Own Health Care," Forbes.com, November 18, 2011.

might help. Michelson told me I would have to handle all the logistics; my father wouldn't have the energy. Dad's one job was to fight and survive the beast. He warned me that highly successful people often don't look after their health—they think they are invincible. I knew I needed to take control, with Michelson and his company as my quarterback. I was excited. As soon as I got off the phone, I told Dad that we had a team in our corner—a strong team; he sighed and said, "Okay, let's do this." Over the following few months, we saw positive progress, and the nurses and doctors at the Mayo Clinic couldn't believe how much Dad had improved. He didn't look like the same person who had shown up looking like he was literally at death's door. Dad always gave them the same line: "I'm above the grass; that's all that counts."

From my perspective, once the oncologists gave us a solid game plan, I felt relief. There was hope, at least.

The following two years and change were a roller coaster of emotion. My father had watched his own father die of lung cancer after five years of treatment. So, my dad never really trusted doctors and regularly cheated on his medication. Frustrated, I took greater control and attended every doctor's appointment. I organized his medication regimen and started a binder for lab reports, doctor's reports, pharmaceutical information, receipts, and miscellaneous notes. It was hard for Dad. He had always been in control; he was the boss, everyone relied on him, and he was very hands-on. I remember we fought like children once; I said, "I'm in control; I'm in charge," and he said, "Oh no you are not." Baby Stacey had grown up. Eventually, Dad said to Keith, "I don't want her to be in control, but I know she has to be." Finally, he let me take over.

In the early days, he was embarrassed. Prostate cancer is a personal disease, so I often left the room when things got too intimate. As time went on, those boundaries became less important. I remember once Dad said, "I used to change her diapers!" pointing at me and laughing, trying to level the playing field just a little.

I felt extremely vulnerable during this period. I had been entrusted with Dad's health and his fight for life; I had to be on my A game. I was nurse, scheduler, confidant, friend, daughter, and comforter. Keith took over the dental business's books and the practice manager role from me. I hired people to cover my hygiene responsibilities. Keith's parents and my Auntie Barb and Uncle Brian stepped up to look after the children. My life became all about my father—but we were in this together.

The Mayo Clinic's treatment plan took effect, and Dad's PSA levels dropped from "jumbo jet" to fifty-three, a lot less scary. Private Health conducted extensive research and suggested we go to The University of Texas MD Anderson Cancer Center in Houston, the highest-rated cancer hospital in the United States. We arrived in September 2014 and met with Dr. Chu, who immediately started Dad on chemotherapy and medication for the bone pain he was suffering. We traveled to Houston once a month through August 2015, flying down in Dad's plane or taking a commercial flight from Williston. On one occasion, Dad's pilot made a rough landing in Houston, and Dad commented that it felt like they were landing a WWII bomber.

Dr. Chu told us he had never seen such aggressive cancer. In between trips to Houston, we went to the Trinity CancerCare Center in Minot, North Dakota, weekly for six courses of radium treatment. While we attended the MD Anderson Cancer Center, we took some time off and visited the Space Center. Dad was fascinated by the massive collection of space suits and chunks of the moon. The International Space Station Gallery was one of our favorites; it allowed us to see "inside" the space station. I hadn't realized it was almost as long as a football field. It was so good to see Dad's mind taken off his illness during these brief interludes of "normal" life.

Normal also meant visiting our beloved Whitefish with Dad's brother and sister, Barb, Norma, Keith, and the kids. I remember we went whitewater rafting. Although Dad didn't join us, he lived it vicariously through the tons of photographs we took. We also spent time at the lake house. Dad spent a lot of time fishing and boating with Garrett and Katie. It felt like it might last forever, but we eventually had to head back to Minnesota for more treatment.

In August 2014, Keith, I, and the kids took the opportunity to have our annual medical appointments at the Mayo Clinic. We stayed at a condo attached to the clinic; it saved us from having to leave the building for Dad's treatments. We tried to build some fun and entertainment into these hospital visits. We all loved to eat at the famous, family-run Canadian Honker Restaurant (named after the Canada goose) in Rochester. There was an open market within walking distance, and we went to a summer festival. No matter how bad things get, finding a way to live in the moment and not get sucked into a self-pitying vortex of despair is crucial.

At the end of 2014, Dad went to Cabo San Lucas, Mexico, with Norma, which gave me some respite. However, losing control over his care was stressful. Despite the disease, he still wanted to enjoy his retirement as best he could.

Private Health continued to work away in the background and came up with an out-of-the-box option: immunotherapy. This treatment attempts to boost the body's cancer-fighting defenses, allowing one's immune system to attack the cancer cells better. We headed to Johns Hopkins Cancer Center in Baltimore, Maryland, for this treatment. In September 2015, Dr. Ken prescribed OPDIVO but needed Dad to complete his radium treatments first.

Still Working

Dad was still working while we traveled from hospital to hospital and back and forth to the US His so-called retirement was a bit of a sham. He'd stayed on officially as a consultant after the sale, but for all intents and purposes, he was still running the business with Kent, the operations manager. Wherever we were, when he was strong enough, Dad would always be on the phone; the company was his life. I remember once he was so sick he couldn't walk, but he still managed a conference call for work.

He'd go into the office every morning when we were back in Saskatchewan. It was a thirty-minute drive from the lake house to Lampman, and Dad insisted on driving himself. I had a secret arrangement with the employees at the office. They would call me and tell me when he arrived and left so I could keep tabs on him. He still had the old family home in Lampman, next door to the business, so he sometimes went there for a nap when he got too tired. Fighting cancer and the ravages of the treatments took its toll. Looking back, it was amazing he managed to do as much as he did. He even played golf; Norma had encouraged him to take up the hobby. For someone given only four months to live, he was giving it his best shot at taking it one day at a time.

It was January 2016 before we returned to Johns Hopkins for a six-week series of treatments. Dad and I used to go to the movie theater across the street every weekend. I remember seeing *The Revenant* (Dad loved that it was filmed partly in Alberta), *13 Hours: The Secret Soldiers of Benghazi,* and *Dirty Grandpa.* Dad felt that the latter, roundly panned by critics, was not something to which he should have taken his daughter. That made me laugh—not the movie, but his comment. We both loved movies, popcorn with butter, and Coca-Cola. We had always been close, but we became even closer during the months he fought for his life.

We talked about Mom and Clinton, his grandkids, and, of course, work. We'd see his HG pumpjacks everywhere when we traveled to Minot for treatment. Once, I asked Dad if he realized the impact he had made on the landscape and the oil industry. He thought about it for a while and said, "You know, Stacey, I've never really thought about it; I always just loved what I did." Then we'd talk about his dad and the legacy he had left and Grandpa's unimpeachable integrity. His father had once said, "You might as well tell the truth, son, because a liar can never keep track of all his lies." The Grimes family excelled at delivering excellent customer service because they genuinely cared about people.

We worked out a way to constantly be in each other's company. We learned to recognize when we needed space, peace, quiet, or time to think. I think I learned how to grieve, or perhaps at least prepare myself for the grief to come. There is a difference between having someone snatched from you on a dark and foggy night and having time to come to terms with losing someone— with the latter, you have the opportunity to form a bond that survives death.

Keith and the kids joined us for a visit and stayed for a week. We rented a car and drove to Washington, DC. We drove past the White House, another bucket list item of Dad's. It was so much larger than we expected. One of the highlights of Dad's last two years of life was visiting the Smithsonian National Air and Space Museum—he was passionate about aircraft and flying. Against his wishes, I rented him a mobility scooter, and he was mad at me at first, refusing to use it, but in the end, he relented and it enabled him to see all the exhibits without getting too tired. He thanked me later. It was a joy to see him enthralled by Amelia Earhart's Lockheed Vega 5B, the plane in which she flew across the Atlantic Ocean. I like to think he was imagining making that flight himself. We visited the National Aquarium in Baltimore's Inner Harbor the following day. We were surprised to see Vice President Joe Biden with his grandchildren wandering around the exhibits, followed closely by bodyguards.

We initially stayed at the Four Seasons Hotel, where some pre–Democratic Convention meetings were being held, so it was fun to play "Spot the Famous Politician." We only stayed for about a week at the hotel while looking for somewhere better suited to our needs. Toward the end of our stay, Dad suffered side effects from the immunotherapy drugs, including running a fever. He was shivering and felt awful, so we couldn't go out for food. It was scary because he looked so desperately ill. The staff at the hotel were excellent and looked after our every need. Once his fever broke, he felt better, and I remember him saying, "My God, Stacey, I never want to go through that again."

The treatment at Johns Hopkins was tough on Dad; he'd go every day or sometimes every other day. When he wasn't at the hospital, he spent a lot of time in bed. We rented an apartment in Spinnaker Bay at Harbor East overlooking the water. It was next to the fabulous Oceanaire Seafood Room, and there was a Whole Foods next door. Dad loved the stew from the nearby James Joyce Irish Pub, and we'd order it regularly. He would sit for hours watching the boats and the activity around the harbor.

Much later, when I was reminiscing with Jackie, Dad's office manager, she told me that he often talked about the Baltimore trip. She said he especially enjoyed visiting Fort McHenry, famous during the War of 1812 for protecting Baltimore's Inner Harbor from the invading British army in 1814. I remember Dad and Garrett wandering around the national monument discussing the war and Fort McHenry's involvement—grandfather and grandson, history buffs together.

These are some of my most cherished memories. When helping a loved one navigate a terminal illness, it is crucial to give them time away from the disease. They may only represent brief moments of respite, but these precious, concentrated moments of life remind them that they are still alive. One of the few tangible gifts you can give someone staring their mortality in the face is to help them live in the present moment.

Dad Beats Prostate Cancer, But . . .

Dr. Ken at Johns Hopkins suggested that Dad try a particular treatment unavailable in America. Taking his advice, we traveled to Germany to see Dr. Baum at the Zentralklinik in Bad Berka, a spa town eighty-four miles southwest of Leipzig.

We didn't think anything of traveling 4,500 miles for treatment. When buying time for someone you love, all other considerations are insignificant. We arrived in early March and stayed ten days at a spa and golf resort in Weimar near the clinic. Dad received PSMA-targeted radioligand therapy (PSMA-RLT) for six days, an experimental radium treatment for progressive, hormone-resistant prostate cancer.

The Central Clinic (Zentralklinik) is in a vast, impressive, state-of-the-art hospital in a complex of medical buildings. At its heart is a massive atrium with a restaurant and information touchscreens and other incredible technology. To be honest, it makes our Canadian facilities look second-rate. The original clinic on the site was built in the early 1950s and treated tuberculosis. Today, it is a leader in treating this evil, progressive, and sly disease.

On March 14, Dr. Baum ordered a whole-body PET/CT scan using gallium-68 PSMA, a radioactive tracer. Dad's body lit up like a Christmas tree. Here is an excerpt from the radiologist's report.

Innumerable, intense PSMA-positive bone and bone marrow metastases are present in the skull, vertebral column, ribs, pelvis, and proximal extremities.

Multiple PSMA-avid lymph node metastases are noted extending from the supraclavicular and paratracheal region to the retroperitoneum (left paraaortic) and along the iliac chains as well as in the inguinal region.

There are several soft tissue metastases present as well.

There is no evidence of residual disease in the prostate gland or any organ metastases in the liver or lungs.

The ironic thing from the report above is that there was no evidence of residual disease in the prostate gland. Dr. Baum was clear that had the prostate cancer been discovered before it had a chance to spread to Dad's liver, the prognosis would have been so much better. Early detection is crucial; I firmly believe that every man should get a physical exam and a PSA test annually. If my father had taken these precautions, the outcome would have been very different.

In between trips to Germany, Dad continued his regular chemotherapy treatments at the Trinity CancerCare Center in Minot. He continued with the treatments until shortly before he died.

We returned to Zentralklinik for a second round of

treatment in May of that year. During periods when Dad was feeling up to it, we managed to see a little of the town. It was an attractive place with a river running through it. The famous novelist, poet, and playwright Goethe had lived there, and his restored summerhouse is open to the public.

Dad's last treatment with Dr. Baum was on July 19, 2016. Luckily, he suffered no adverse effects from the therapy. On this visit, we received both positive and worrying news. Dad's bone metastases had reduced by 50 percent, and there was talk of partial remission. But Dad had lost over seventeen pounds in the previous two months and needed regular blood transfusions. They gave him three units of blood. Back at the hotel, we did what we loved most: watch movies, which I had downloaded to my computer before we left home. By this stage, Dad was too weak to play golf, even though there was a course right outside our door. I watched while he weighed himself every day. He was wasting away, and it was heartbreaking. There wasn't much to make us smile, but a golf tournament was in progress one day, and I noticed my name in giant letters. The sponsor was Wempe Watches—Dad joked that Keith and I were famous. He got a kick out of that.

Garrett and Katie joined Dad and me on that trip to Germany. Time with his grandchildren was valuable, and it was running out. There had been a marked deterioration in

Dad's health since our previous visit. However, Dad was still upbeat, and the nurses and doctors were amazed by how he coped with the pain of extensive cancer in his bones. When asked, he would simply say, "I'm grateful to still be alive." He was a tenacious fighter, and he rose to every medical challenge thrown at him.

The kids had a lot of fun despite the circumstances and, of course, were being fed only vague information about Grandpa's illness and treatment. We visited Erfurt, the capital of the region in which we were located. It is a beautiful city with many squares, markets, and history at every turn. Garrett and Dad loved the old abbey, the cathedral with its fifteenth-century stained glass, and the Baroque city fortress. Katie and I loved the Merchants' Bridge; it was one of our favorite places. It has half-timbered houses on it and crosses the river. The decorative house timbers are painted green, brown, red, and blue; at the end, one house is painted emerald green. The bridge enjoys the honor of being the longest medieval bridge to still have people living in the houses above it. The upper levels are apartments; at street level, there are boutiques, art galleries, specialty food stores, and more.

We also went to Weimar, historically significant because of the Weimar Republic, which lasted until 1933 and was culturally significant as the intellectual center of Germany in the late 1700s and early 1800s. There were several castles, museums, churches, the Liszt House and Museum, and many charming city squares.

We were scheduled to return for what they called restaging and Dad's fourth PSMA-RLT on November 21, 2016—an appointment he would never make.

On Monday, October 10, 2016, we celebrated Thanksgiving with Dad's sister Barb, brother-in-law Brian, and nephews and nieces. Auntie Barb cooked turkey, Dad's favorite cabbage rolls, and all the traditional fixings. He was in a great mood; he ate well and told jokes. He brought a case of Bud Light, his favorite beverage.

We made one more trip to Minot for chemotherapy about ten days later, but there was a marked difference in Dad's bearing. The smiling, joking Thanksgiving Dad had disappeared. He had begun to experience numbness and tingling on his left side and had difficulty moving his hands. It was the beginning of Dad's final chapter.

CHAPTER TEN

The Final Chapter

Dad had called and asked Keith to take him to the house in Lampman and mentioned that his right hand was now numb. Over the previous few days, he had complained he was experiencing some numbness in his face and asked Keith to check his teeth. Keith took X-rays, but they didn't show any dental issues. On Saturday, November 5, 2016, Dad fell; he was at the house in Lampman. I somehow knew the cancer had spread to his brain.

On Monday, four weeks after Thanksgiving, I insisted he go and see the doctor. You probably know what happened next—he insisted on driving. He was swerving all over the road; it was frightening. When I mentioned it, he said, "Well, you're going to put me in the hospital anyway!" I think he knew this would be his last trip to the hospital—and the last time he would drive. We got there in one piece, but not before the conversation also veered off, and he said, "Stacey, I don't want a funeral. You'll probably give me one anyway, but I don't want one." I promised him I would not go against his wishes. He continued, as if he hadn't heard me, "I want a celebration of life. And you mustn't cry. I don't want you to be sad. I've had a wonderful life; your mom and I raised two great kids, and you gave us two beautiful and healthy grand-children. Mom, Clinton, and I were successful in business—we did well." I was fighting back the tears. He said, "I want a marquee in the yard at Lampman, just like the one we had at your wedding. I want a ton of KFC for people to eat. And it needs to be held a little before the May long weekend. The farmers will be out seeding, and I don't want to spoil anyone's time off." But I'm getting ahead of myself.

He was admitted to the hospital in Estevan. The doctor ordered a CT scan. Amazingly, tiny St. Joseph's Hospital, with less than one hundred beds, has a state-of-the-art scanner. In 2016, my father donated one hundred thousand dollars to the fundraising campaign; now, he was a beneficiary of having this machine in our community. What is it they say about karma?

I'd popped home for supper and a shower and was just about to return when the doctor called me to tell me the scan results. I was correct; the cancer had moved inexorably to his brain. I asked the doctor whether he had to give my dad the results; he said that my father had asked him for the results, and he had to tell him the truth. Shortly after, Dad called me and told me the news. His voice breaking, he said, "Stacey, what do I do?" By this time, he was used to me handling everything, but I was at the end of my emotional tether, and so a bland, noncommittal statement was all I could manage: "Dad, we'll just take it one day at a time."

He was in a lot of pain, and so I stayed with him day and night save for brief respites for meals. I called the family, all of them, and his friends and employees. Dad was much loved. It became a pilgrimage; everyone who loved him came to say their last goodbyes, including many children. He loved kids—especially, of course, his grandchildren. A contingent from Schlumberger in Calgary arrived, including Gier, who managed Dad's business during the transition period. Coincidentally, he died of a brain tumor the following year.

I don't know how I would have coped if it had happened four years later during the pandemic. Those who loved Dad wouldn't have been able to say their goodbyes, which would have destroyed him and broken my heart. During his final five days, he drifted in and out of consciousness. Norma and I stayed by his side, holding his hands; I slept in a cot beside his bed. And then his breathing became labored, and I knew it was time. I told him he had fought a hard battle for two and a half years, and it was okay now to leave us. I had called the hospital priest, who was there to give Dad his last rites. His brother Gary and his family; his sisters, Barbara, Judy, and Karen; his grandchildren; Norma; Keith; and I held him as he took his last breath.

All Alone

I felt like an orphan; Mom, Dad, and Clinton were all gone. I was all alone, or at least that's how it felt. Of course, I still had Keith and the kids, and all my aunts, uncles, and cousins, and I loved them all. But the family I had been born into, my immediate family, was all gone. Once again, the anger returned. *Why didn't Dad go to the doctor earlier?*

It sounds awful, but I had a more challenging time with Dad's death than Mom's. Mom had been the glue that held our family together, and Dad took over that role when she died. It was like Dad was a backup parent. For a year after Mom died, we spoke or texted most days, especially when he was traveling. Now who would I call several times a week? My support system had disappeared, and I felt alone. I missed Dad's words of wisdom, such as, "You will get up at the same time tomorrow, and the sun will shine the same as it did today." Another one of his "kick-up-the-butt" sayings was,

"Stacey, there is always a solution to any problem; you just have to give it enough thought and come up with it." Of course, the sun doesn't always shine; sometimes, the day is dark and dismal. And sometimes, there simply isn't a solution; I couldn't bring him back to life. However, I could find a way through my grief.

I took solace in the fact that we went through his fight with cancer together. We had a lot of time together to talk, reminisce, have in-depth discussions, laugh, cry, and become closer than I ever thought possible. I cherish the months and years I got to spend with my father. We experienced every second, minute, hour, and day as if it were our last—because we only have today. Yesterday is past; we can't do anything to change it. Tomorrow has yet to happen. So we live in the only reality we have—this moment.

I could have sat and grieved, locking myself away emotionally and physically. It would have been easy. I'd done it before. This time was different. I'd spent the last couple of years of my life with Dad giving him the gift of more time, fighting the battle by his side every step of the way. We'd talked everything out; nothing was left to say to each other. I felt a sense of closure that I had not experienced when Clinton and Mom passed. A week after Dad died, it was the birthday of my best friend, Karyse, and we took our daughters to Regina on a Christmas shopping trip. We stayed in a nice hotel, ate good food, shopped until we dropped, and even went to the waterslides. It felt good, we had fun, and for those few days, I didn't dwell on Dad's passing. He would have smiled and said, "Go for it, girl!" After a week of mourning I went back to work part-time.

Of course, my life is never simple; drama lurks on the horizon. It was snowing when we got back to Estevan, and I told Karyse I would get Keith to pick me up at her house. That way, she wouldn't have to drive further than necessary in the awful weather. My friend Tamara lives next door to Karyse, and when she saw us pull up, she came out to hug me. In the process, I slipped on the ice, fell, and hit my head on the pavement. I ended up in the hospital—the last place I wanted to see again so soon. The hospital intern said I was okay, but I knew I wasn't. Eventually, I was diagnosed with post-concussion syndrome. The fall had also pulled my body out of alignment, not for the first time, so I was a regular at my chiropractor's office for the next twelve months. I soldiered on, which is what you do—or at least what I did, given I didn't have a choice.

I was embroiled in dealing with Dad's estate in the first months of the new year. In January, I found a buyer for the house in Lampman, my childhood home. It would have been more of a challenge parting with the bricks and mortar that held so many memories if not for the fact that the buyer was one of Dad's employees. A bonus was that his wife had often visited Mom in her greenhouse across from Grimes Sales and Service. Mom had taken Tammy under her wing and taught her about growing plants and vegetables. I knew the house would be well looked after and new family memories would be made there.

However, I had to clear out a lifetime of memories before the new buyers could take possession of the house. It was the same feeling I later experienced in my garage, opening Clinton's trunk. Every Friday, I would trek over to the house and sift through my parents' life, drawer by drawer, box by box. I felt like an interloper and expected them to step into the room at any moment and ask me what the heck I was doing. It took me over five months to clear out the house, but I never had the courage to open the trunk. When you consider that Dad had moved into the lake house several years before he died, it was surprising I still managed to take away twelve large totes of things from the Lampman house that I couldn't bear to throw out. It's odd the things one can't part with: Mom's fur coat, my walking dolls from childhood. Everything else was redistributed throughout the town and beyond through multiple garage sales. I like to think that there's a little of Mom, Dad, and Clinton in hundreds of houses in Lampman and Estevan.

In March 2017, the tears came in torrents, accompanied by severe bouts of anxiety; my whole body felt on high alert. I couldn't sleep. I spiraled out of control and was constantly triggered by little things. I'd get upset with our employees at the clinic, or with the kids and Keith. The clinic was too much for me. I knew enough by this time to seek help, so I brought in a specialist transition team. I'd used them in the past, and after we moved our clinic across the city, they helped me develop systems for the new clinic. Standing in the clinic, I took a metaphorical step back and asked myself what sort of leader I wanted to be—how did I want to lead? I had built quite a support team around me, and I leaned heavily on them. I was growing, and my actions brought me back from the brink. That was progress.

I knew I needed a break—we, as a family, needed a break. A month before Dad's memorial, we went on a Disney cruise to the Caribbean. I switched off and didn't think about Dad's estate, the memorial, or anything else; I just spent time with my husband and children. Travel can be a powerful restorative—sometimes, you must escape and regroup. We sat on beaches, met Mickey and Goofy, and watched a *Pirates of the Caribbean* parade. We celebrated Katie's fourteenth birthday, and it was perfect—almost.

I became fully immersed in organizing Dad's memorial when we got back. And what a celebration it was.

A Celebration of Life

We held Dad's celebration of life in May 2017, and it was exactly as he had wanted. It was a celebration of Mom's and Clinton's lives too. Dad had said he didn't want a funeral, and we honored his wishes. However, we did hold a graveside service just before the celebration of life. Everyone met at the Grimes Sales and Service shop, and we took buses to the church. Two hundred people attended. It was a windy but not unpleasant day, and the priest delivered a beautiful service. There were laughter and tears and a whole lot of stories. One of our clinic employees, Laura, who plays in a pipe-band, played "Amazing Grace" on the bagpipes. It was one of Dad's favorite pieces. When I was clearing out his desk, I found Duke's ashes. Duke was my parent's German wirehaired pointer and a faithful companion; he liked to hang out with Dad and Clinton. My cousin Kirk placed Duke's ashes next to Dad's in the ground. Dad would have liked that.

At the celebration of life, the tent was huge. Over five hundred people turned out to see Dad off in style. The theme was black and white—a symphony of elegance. A passerby could easily have mistaken it for a wedding, except for the KFC—Dad would have been so pleased. We had music and a bar, and everyone had an opportunity to flip through the photo books I'd made showcasing Clinton's, Mom's, and Dad's lives. The journey back in time was bittersweet for many, and as they turned the pages, there were smiles, sadness, and fondness as memories came flooding back.

The flower arrangements on every table were made by my friend Trina Whelan, who owns a florist shop called A Loving Touch in Estevan. The flowers were bright blue, yellow, white, pink, and purple, all spring colors. Mom's favorite, pussy willow, was prevalent, as were cotton flower and *Oncidium* orchids. The flowers were arranged in my mother's vases and antique pottery. Mom loved restoring antique "treasures." We often found her stripping the paint or varnish off a soon-to-be-refurbished piece. I remember once when a customer was in the office wanting to pay his bill. He caught the tail end of a conversation between my mother and her best friend, Bev. Bev had just asked Mom what she was doing over the weekend, and Mom replied, "Stripping." The look on the customer's face was priceless—everyone broke down in laughter.

In the tent, a banner with Dad's photograph in the foreground read, "Forever in our Hearts, Melvyn Grimes,

1947–2016." The background photo was an HG pumpjack. A professional photographer recorded the day. Looking back at the more than three hundred images the photographer took, one thing stands out: all the smiling faces. Dad would have liked that. Dad's good friend Ray Frehlich spoke about how incredibly ethical Dad was in business and talked about his generous and continuous support for the community. Norma's son-in-law, Nick, gave a beautiful speech about Dad's impact on their family and how much fun he was. Keith spoke about how Dad, Mom, and Clinton always welcomed him as one of the family, and he mentioned how touched he was by Dad's toast to us at our wedding. He also recalled the support he always got from my dad, who gave him a summer job at the shop so he could afford to go back to dental school. At the end of his speech, Keith turned to look at me and thanked me for caring for Dad during his long fight with cancer and for looking after him and Katie and Garrett. Finally, he acknowledged the courage it must have taken. I felt a sense of validation, which eased my guilt about being away so much on what felt like a medical pilgrimage.

Finally, I looked out at over five hundred faces from a town with a population of a little over seven hundred souls. It struck me how my father and our family had impacted this little corner of Saskatchewan. When it was my time to speak, I didn't really offer a eulogy in the true sense but instead spoke from the heart about Dad's life, his parents, his school days (he used to say if he'd spent less time in pool halls, he would have gotten better grades), his talent for math, and his fear of dentists. I talked about his career and his care and compassion for people and community, his philanthropy, and his love for his employees, who were like family to him.

The mood changed a little during the memorial presentation. The photographs taken that day tell the story; people were focused intently on the screen, many with hands to their faces, trying not to shed tears. There is a photo of Garrett wearing a suit and sitting next to Katie, who looks demure in a simple black dress; Garrett's eyes are closed, and his fingertips are rubbing his temples. He looks inconsolable, another poor soul ill-equipped to deal with loss and grief. The montage of photographs playing onscreen silenced the room. Together, we remembered happier times; individually, we struggled with our emotions.

Several years earlier, I had given Dad some personalized golf balls as a Christmas gift; for years afterward, people would tell him that they'd found one of his balls in a tree or in the bushes. He always laughed and said, "Yep, I don't have the best swing." In memory of this, everyone who attended the celebration of life received a box of memorial golf balls. Many people subsequently played a round of golf with those balls in memory of Dad. I imagine some of those balls are still turning up in strange places on the local course, reminding the finder of Melvyn Grimes, a Lampman legend: "In Loving Memory of Melvyn Grimes: February 2, 1947–November 15, 2016."

Choices

By late spring, the chickens were coming home to roost. Katie was having a tough time dealing with Dad's death. She was hurting. I had been away more than I'd been at home for the previous two years, failing to give her the emotional support she needed. Keith had done his best, but he had the business to run, and Katie needed her mother. I had tried to make it work by taking the kids with me whenever feasible and spending quality time with them between trips, but it was not enough—how could it have been? I suppose I had been so wrapped up in keeping Dad alive that I'd failed to notice how much it was affecting the children, especially Katie.

A friend suggested I check out a program called Choices, which she had taken over a decade earlier. Choices was founded by a woman named Thelma Box. I visited the website and read that it was "a unique personal development program that leads you through a journey of visiting experiences in the past, evaluating current circumstances, and making new choices about what your future will be."[1] My friend had thought the program would help me, but when I told her that I felt it was Katie who needed help, she told me they offered a weeklong teen camp.

Before Katie could attend the teen camp, it was a prerequisite that at least one parent attend a preparatory Choices program. I attended my weekend course in July, and Katie went to teen camp for a week in August.

During the Choices Givers II program, I remember creating what they called a contract, which was more of a declaration. It was: "I am a passionate, free woman." One of my homework exercises was to list ten times I had felt like a winner or done things where I felt proud. Graduating school, college, and life coaching were in the mix, as was giving birth to Garrett and Katie and looking after my parents during their illnesses. When the critter in your head is harping on about everything you have done wrong in your life, it's easy to forget about all the good you have done and achieved, but it's important not to lose sight of your achievements. There were other questions: *What do you want people to remember about you? What do you want*

---

1 https://choicesseminars.com/seminars/

to accomplish before you die? Interestingly, they also asked, *What would the title be if a book were written about you?* At the time, I wrote *"Resilient."*

I remember being angry during that time—mad at the world, still furious that Clinton had left me. Every time I thought I'd expunged the anger from my soul, it bounced back with a vengeance.

During the teen week, the kids at the camp discovered who they were and what they wanted out of this stage of their lives. They were given the tools to communicate more effectively with their parents. They discovered how to manage self-doubt, ask for help, and recognize the self-defeating things they did that complicated their lives. I recently looked back at Katie's notes; she'd listed three things she needed from me and three from her dad—tough things that cut to the bone. Our behavior at the time was detrimentally affecting her. But then she'd also listed the things she liked/loved about us, which were heartwarming. At the bottom of the page, she'd completed the following: "My contract and purpose is: I am a strong and passionate young lady."

The final stage of the program was for Keith and me to join Katie for the last three days of the camp. It was a fantastic experience. We got to work together as a team and get on the same page. There were about forty of us there, all told. Everyone was figuring out how to make their family more robust and improve their home lives. There were group sessions during which the teens confronted their parents about their feelings. For instance, they would say things like, "I wish you didn't fight as much" or "You need to be more present for me." Hearing my fourteen-year-old daughter say, "We need to do better as a family" and "I want you to be less angry" was a humbling experience. There wasn't a dry eye in the house. It was a pivotal growth moment for everyone, especially for us.

I went back in October and took another Choices program. It helped me understand that I was responsible for writing my own life script and could edit it anytime. Simple, but wow!

Dad's Estate

Despite all the life challenges I was facing then, I still had to deal with Dad's estate. It took me almost two years to sort out his life and business, or maybe *dismantle* might be a better word. Although he had sold the company, there were still ties; he could never sever the umbilical cord completely. When the company's future was threatened a few years later, I discovered how inextricably connected my family was to the business.

For now, I was thankful that Dad had put a trusted lawyer, banker, and accountant in place to work with me. During all those months when Dad and I were traveling from hospital to hospital and he was undergoing new and groundbreaking treatments, he never let me see fully behind the curtain regarding his assets. Sure, I knew he'd sold the business and owned two homes and an airplane, but I soon discovered he owned property I had never heard of, four cars, and a bunch of other stuff.

I reread my material on the wheel of fear and decided that the only way to manage this enormous task was to be organized and rely heavily on the team Dad had put in place. The first thing I did was to buy a huge binder! My primary objective was to avoid making bad decisions. As mentioned earlier, Dad had always considered me his baby girl—even after I became a mother. Things changed in the two years before his death. He began to lean on me heavily, and it became apparent that I had become the grown-up in the relationship out of necessity. However, he still tried to protect his "baby girl" from the mean old world.

In the beginning, I questioned my ability to handle Dad's estate. However, I worked it out, and I think he would have been proud of me. Mom and Clinton would have been proud too.

Life Goes On—Sometimes Smoothly, Sometimes Not

Dealing with Dad's lawyer, accountant, and bank manager, while at the same time taking more interest in managing the practice, helped my confidence grow. It allowed me to continue with my life; there was just a ton more to do. I fought fires, dealt with toxic people, laughed, cried, and hugged my kids, Keith, and many long-standing patients. I knew Dad wouldn't have wanted me to be sad, but some days I felt down for no apparent reason. It took me a while, but I realized that my subconscious was registering significant dates, even if I hadn't consciously realized it was the anniversary of someone's death or birthday. I've lost a lot of people during my fifty or so years: friends, relatives, and soulmates—there are a lot of dates on the calendar that are forever tinged with sadness. I allowed myself to cry and to grieve and, more surprisingly, to laugh. Unfortunately, it wasn't enough.

In the spring of 2018, I was diagnosed with moderate to severe anxiety and started therapy again. Initially, doctors medicated me with Ativan, which I'd taken for two weeks after Clinton's death, but a nurse practitioner specializing in mental health in Minot prescribed the antidepressant amitriptyline, which helped me manage my mood swings and sleep better. I'd stopped taking Wellbutrin way back in 2005.

Counseling helped too. The simple opportunity of talking about situations that trigger panic attacks was a huge benefit. But it was cognitive behavioral therapy (CBT) that helped me recognize those triggers and gave me the tools to manage situations before they got out of control. CBT focuses on what symptoms you are experiencing in the moment, not the cause of your anxiety. It allows you to recognize how your thoughts, behaviors, and emotions affect how you feel and behave. How you perceive a situation (a trigger) directly affects your feelings, affecting your response.

A friend of mine explained that while driving, he would get frustrated and angry every time he came to a red traffic light. He would thump the steering wheel and complain that the universe was against him. He knew this was ridiculous, even childish, but he couldn't prevent those red lights (the situation) from triggering negative thoughts and emotions that resulted in a hissy fit. His CBT therapist suggested reframing the situation so that catching traffic lights at red became a positive event. She suggested he use the thirty-to-sixty-second wait wait at a red light to carry out a mini meditation: simply focus on his breath for that short period and enjoy a moment of peace. To help the effectiveness of this tool, he began leaving for appointments five minutes earlier. This strategy lessened concerns about being late, which was part of his anxiety. He told me that it wasn't long before he looked forward to a traffic light turning red in front of him; he looked forward to his minute or so of calm.

Cognitive behavioral therapy has taught me that I have a choice as to whether I let loose on someone or reframe the situation so that it doesn't trigger me in the first place. Using this tool has helped me to control my temper. I realize now that I don't become overwhelmed if I take inventory of what I need to deal with and then prioritize that list. Previously, I'd let every little thing bother me, and I'd spiral out of control. Another challenge was that I often felt I wasn't being heard. The tool I used to overcome this was to acknowledge the other person's position when I disagreed with them, but at the same time clearly state my position. In that way, I knew I was being heard, which allowed me to let things go.

During this period, I also practiced yoga and walked a lot. I find yoga relaxing—so much so that if I have the opportunity, I can sleep for a couple of hours after a session. Like CBT, it helps me reframe my thinking and focus on the symptoms rather than the root cause. To this day, if I am

Spending time with Uncle Gary, Auntie Bev, Kirk, and Kevin

Kathy and Clinton on the trail ride

Keith's
high school
graduation

75th Anniversary parade of Lampman

Clinton and I as a junior bridesmaid and groomsman
at Keith and Carla's wedding

Senior
graduation
picture with
Grandma
Mayer

Keith and I
at my high school
graduation

BELOW:
Minot State
graduation

Our wedding day

Exchanging our
vows and rings

My favorite picture of Mom and me

Dad and me at the wedding

Top: The groomsmen at our wedding
Above: The grandparents having fun at the wedding

Family picture at Whitefish

Marsha, Clinton, Dad, and me at Whitefish

Uncle Jack and Aunt Jean

Mom meeting Garrett for the first time

Mom an Dad at the Great Wall of China

Uncle Kirby and
Auntie Rachelle

Below:
Grandma Elaine,
Grandpa Al,
and Garrett

Garrett and Dutchie

Left:
Grandpa Mel
rocking Garrett

Keith and
Garrett
at Whitefish

Our family
is complete
with Katie

BELOW:
Mom,
Garrett,
and Katie

Mom cooking
with Katie

Going to Disneyworld

Right: Loving spending time with the cousins

Below: Grandpa Mel with Garrett and Katie at Garrett's graduation

Katie's graduation

not actively working on myself mentally and physically, I can quickly turn to food for comfort. How easy is it to mindlessly eat an entire pizza instead of a couple of slices that satisfy both your hunger and your craving?

Travel Therapy

In July 2018, we decided to go on another Disney cruise from Barcelona. Among other ports of call, we visited Naples, Livorno, Florence, Pisa, Genoa, and Milan in Italy, as well as Cannes, Monaco, and Marseilles. We were away for three weeks, our longest family vacation.

As I've mentioned, Garrett is a history buff, and we visited almost every historical monument you can imagine—he was in his element. There was plenty of shopping and a full slate of activities, Disney and non-Disney, for the rest of us. Some people may say traveling is a form of escapism and that if you are trying to leave your problems behind, they'll just be there waiting for you when you return. There may be some truth to that, but there is another side of the equation. Traveling allows you to leave your old world behind and focus on who you are with your family—it enables you to get out of your head and into the present moment. Vacations are full of action, stimulation, and excitement, and are, by their very nature, "in the moment." That in itself can offer a valuable respite. The trick is to use the time to regenerate and strengthen yourself so that when you return to the "real world," you can better cope with all that life throws at you.

A therapist once told me, "Traveling helps with grief because it creates new memories." I like that.

Today

As I write this in 2022, I have developed the tools I need to process negative feelings in minutes, or maybe at most an hour. In the past, my mind would run riot; Crazy Clyde, the critter in my head, thrives on drama. He would tell me that I was a failure, an idiot, of no value to society. He would nag at me, preventing me from living in the present moment, keeping me forever tethered to the past. Constantly working on myself, mainly practicing mindfulness and meditation, helps prevent me from drifting toward the dark side. Living for today and not wallowing in the past promotes a healthy lifestyle.

The Choices program and the earlier Fearless Living courses and training helped me reframe the conversation going on in my head. They helped me forgive Clinton, Mom, and Dad for dying and leaving me. They helped me grieve my dad. They helped heal my family.

Writing this book has been a cathartic exercise. It has

allowed me, perhaps forced me, to be vulnerable. I look back to a year ago when I opened Clinton's trunk, and I'm a different person. As Clinton's cologne hit me, I knew I had released more than memories. It was almost like a part of me had been trapped in that box. I had freed myself and could now face the world and tell my story.

I wouldn't want to give the impression that simply writing this book was a cure-all or that my anxiety and depression have disappeared and I no longer feel grief. I still have those emotions; they will always be a part of my identity. However, this exercise has allowed me to release much of the negative emotional energy that has prevented me from living fully for so many years. I can now live in the here and now. I can be present for my family in a way that I found almost impossible in the past, except perhaps for brief periods when the sun broke through the clouds.

As I sit looking out at the lake from my parents' dream house, the grief, loss, and depression are still there, but they no longer have the power to control my life. I am free at last.

Epilogue

Grimes Sales and Service has been an important part of the Lampman community since my grandfather started selling farm implements in the 1940s. He was a councilor for three years and mayor of Lampman for fifteen years and was much respected. In early 1997, as my father, Mel Grimes, groomed his son, Clinton, to take over the business, Lampman residents would have been forgiven for believing that the Grimes legacy was in safe hands. However, Clinton's death changed the family firm's future, and Dad sold the business in March 2014, two days before his prostate cancer diagnosis. That would have ended the family's involvement in the Lampman business if not for a karmic twist of fate.

Grimes Sales and Service Gets a New Owner

Dad always ran the business like a mom-and-pop operation. His employees were like family to him; community meant everything. To say Dad was well respected is an understatement. It didn't sit well that he had sold out, even though he'd done his best to protect everyone's jobs. By staying on in a consulting role, Dad wanted to ensure continuity, but the cancer made this increasingly difficult. Ultimately, Dad's last day of work was one month before he died.

Dad and I often talked about the business when we traveled and hung out at hotels, hospitals, and specialists' offices. He had confided in me that he was concerned Schlumberger might not stay the course. He was, as always, worried about the staff. He had hinted that if things were different, he would have liked to repurchase the business if it ever came up for sale.

My dad's prediction came to pass. In 2020, Schlumberger decided to sell the firm. Oil prices were heading into negative territory; COVID-19 was playing havoc with markets, and the general economy was in the toilet. My dad's employees were in danger of losing their jobs. Twenty members of my dad's "family" were going to be out on the streets; it was an awful situation. All I could think of was how my dad would have felt and what he would have done.

Kent Lees, the longtime manager at my dad's company, approached me and said there was an opportunity to repurchase the business for what would almost be pennies on the dollar. I thought seriously about my options and carried out a cost-benefit analysis. The business was doing well despite the global situation, and Kent offered to invest in it and stay on to run it. Many people advised me against repurchasing it, but it became a no-brainer once I did the math. How could I go wrong with Mom, Dad, and Clinton all whispering in my ear that it was the right thing to do? After all, it was still our family business.

The icing on the cake is that Garrett now works there and loves it. I remember Mom and Dad regularly taking him to the shop when he was younger. When he joined the firm a few years ago, he was warmly welcomed "home" by Dad's well-trained, dedicated team. I'd say that a fourth-generation Grimes family member being part of a company his great-grandfather founded is a beautiful example of the circle of life.

Reconnecting with Marsha

On Thursday, May 14, 2020, I talked to Clinton's former girlfriend, Marsha. My writing coach, Mike, arranged the video call, recorded it, and got it transcribed. Almost two years later, I'm sitting here reviewing the transcript and feel that as my story began with my brother's overwhelming desire to help Marsha, it's only fitting that my final words should be about this remarkable woman. The call was as necessary as opening Clinton's trunk and just as cathartic.

Marsha moved to Calgary after Clinton died and made a new life for herself, but it wasn't easy. Our Zoom call was probably the first time we'd spoken at any length since the day my brother died twenty-seven years earlier. The call lasted nearly three hours, and I discovered much I didn't know about the crash that took my brother: heartbreaking, graphic details that I should have known and dealt with decades ago. New photographic "memories" replaced those that were imagined. The deployed airbags, the way he had been thrown back in his seat, the smashed window—his broken neck. Oh my God.

I hadn't realized Marsha had visited Mom and Dad almost every day in the weeks after the accident and that she kept in touch with them. More importantly, I'd never let myself imagine how she must have felt discovering Clinton's body in the car. Or the unimaginable loss of losing her soulmate. It was wonderful to reconnect with her, but at the same time it was traumatizing to hear about the nightmares she had endured, the help she had needed, and the mental anguish she had suffered.

After Clinton's death, I'd locked myself away with my grief and anger. I hadn't acknowledged the hurt Marsha was feeling. I saw her as the cause of my brother's death, not just another person left behind—a victim like me. I should have been there for her. The tragedy is that she also blamed herself for his death. During the call, Marsha became real to me, and I felt I could finally forgive her, even though there really was nothing to forgive. I could vanquish my own demons and let this woman back into my life. She was graceful, understanding, and forgiving.

We talked about my addiction to grief. Marsha asked me whether I remembered the gift I'd given her for her graduation. I felt guilty that I couldn't remember the locket with Clinton's photograph that she described; I was a zombie back then, but it sounded lovely, and I'm glad I did something nice. She still has it.

I could hear the sadness that was still in her voice. All that pain, all those years lost. I'm glad Marsha and I found each other again, and I can see my brother's true love for what she is and was, not what I had made her out to be in my grief-stricken brain.

What hits me most through the lens of time is that when Clinton died, Marsha was only seventeen years old—the same age Katie is as I write this. I had been angry at a child. I am embarrassed, ashamed, sad. Looking over at Katie, sitting reading on the sofa, I wonder how I could have been so wrapped up in my own grief that I took it out on a child. What's worse, I had not even recognized how devastated Marsha must have been. How selfish I'd been at that moment.

Grief is insidious; it transforms your character, infiltrating your brain like an alien parasite from a science-fiction movie. I do not offer that as an excuse but a reason not to beat yourself up too much for the things you do under the influence of grief. Everyone's grief journey is unique, but rarely is the scenery pretty.

After the call, I remembered the last time I'd spent quality time with Marsha. It was Easter, and we were both in Whitefish a few weeks before the accident. We had so much fun together skiing and talking. It was her first time on the slopes, and she borrowed Mom's skis. The two young lovers talked about her graduation and how she would become an aesthetician. Clinton was so proud to show her off to his family. I remember her laugh, her free spirit, and her kind heart. I knew that as young as they were, Clinton and Marsha were going to get married and have two children, and I'd spend a lot of time hanging out with my sister-in-law and my nephew and niece. I had it all planned out. But it was an illusion.

I will always love Marsha. I will keep in touch with her from this point forward. She was in my brother's life for such a short time, but she made him happy and was a positive influence on his life—I owe her a debt of gratitude. Our conversation dispelled any residual anger; it let me deal with my guilt and hopefully put things right with a seventeen-year-old who asked for help on a foggy night and instead got a lifetime of sadness.

I can now close Clinton's trunk; I have released my demons and dealt with the stuff in my own trunk. The past no longer holds any power over me. I am in control of my destiny and can finally live in the all-powerful present moment.

PART II
Coach's Corner
A Life Coach's Perspective

STEP 1

Discovering the
Real You

AFTER LOOKING BACK on the events described in this book, I
offer the following observations. Please note that not all chap-
ters have notes. I hope my thoughts, comments, and mean-
derings in this section will provide a deeper look into my frame
of mind at the time and what, in retrospect, I learned along the
way. They are, inevitably, tempered by the sands of time.

You will also find life-coaching advice based on my training
and experience as a CFLC and what worked for me then.

At the end of each section, you will find a list of "points
to ponder." These are not meant to be exercises or a test; feel
free to use them as stepping stones to help you gain new
perspectives on your emotional standing by answering these
probing questions and doing the exercises. These questions
are intended to help you take stock of where you are on
your personal journey of grief. I pray they might help you

rediscover the real you, the one lying beneath the layers of hurt and guilt, the things said and unsaid.

Considering these questions and keeping a journal of my answers and thoughts brought the real me back to my family and friends. I encourage you to sit with these questions for a while and maybe write your own answers, thoughts, and feelings down in your journal. Always remember, this is your journey; it is unique to you.

Opening the Box

I hope you can learn from my example. For a long time, I never wanted to know the details of Clinton's accident. I didn't want to know how Clinton was hurt. I couldn't visit the accident site and look at his truck because I didn't want to know what he'd had to endure. The questions overwhelmed me. Did he suffer? Did he know what was happening? Why didn't he hear the train? At the viewing, all I can remember were the bumps and bruises on his face. I remember I touched his hair. I never asked my parents about what had happened. Only when I decided to write this book did I ask Marsha to tell me all the details, in a call that lasted almost three hours.

I hadn't been ready to deal with it before that—it was easier not to know. Coping with grief involves both costs and benefits to your psyche and soul. You have to ask yourself what it is that you fear. This chapter described a small part of my journey; it's important to remember that your journey will be unique to you—there is no right or wrong. I realized the time had come for me to know the truth, the brutal reality, so that I could move on with my life and start remembering the good times we'd had together—all the fun times—without continually playing the "What if?" game.

Opening up Clinton's chest after twenty-three years was probably one of the hardest things I've had to do in a long time. It's easier to just not feel, to hold on to the feelings. Letting yourself feel means being vulnerable. I remember thinking, *What happens if I feel like crying? Is that okay?* And could I show my emotions to my daughter, who filmed the long-awaited revisiting of my brother's death? The answer is yes; showing emotion is healthy. Not only was I able to reconnect with my brother through his posses-sions, but I was also allowed to see how he had seen life as a teenager through looking at his school projects. It took me a long time to overcome my negative nelly attitude, the one that tells you it will be awful, that there's no need, no value—and that's okay. Only you can decide when you are ready to open up and allow a sense of vulnerability into your soul. By opening that long-locked time capsule, I allowed myself to become vulnerable and showed my family that it's okay to be that way.

When it came to it, opening the chest wasn't as scary as I had expected. It's been said that problems and challenges always seem bigger on arrival than on departure. That is so true. The chest was like that. Revisiting Clinton's life meant I had an opportunity to remember all the good times we had together and be grateful for them. In my case, we didn't have a lifetime together, but we packed many good memories into the years we were lucky enough to share.

The less pleasant memories can also flood back when you open that Pandora's box. As I've mentioned, a big one for me was that I never managed to read a eulogy at my brother's funeral. At the time, I was in a daze, so numb it wasn't something I could face. If you have regrets, forgive yourself. No one attending a funeral will think less of the bereaved for failing to give a eulogy or, if you do give one, criticize that it fell short somehow. In my case, eight years later, I visited the site of the accident and read my eulogy to Clinton. I released a balloon and watched it rise into the air just as his soul would have done. Then I went to his grave and left a card there. Small gestures, maybe, but cathartic.

After Clinton's death, I felt great anger toward my brother for leaving me, and I carried a lot of guilt. I asked myself, *How can I bring closure to my feelings of regret and guilt?* As I mentioned earlier, I had to let myself be vulnerable. I finally realized that I had no control over what had happened to my brother. That day, I promised to forgive myself for the regret and culpability I felt around his death. It was time to release that big, black ball of guilt. It had weighed heavy on my soul for far too many years. A sense of calm and peace overcame me as I let it go. At that moment, I knew I was beginning to grieve more healthily.

POINTS TO PONDER

Now, it is your turn to explore your own journey. I suggest making time in your schedule to pause your life and reflect on it. Some people prefer writing in a notebook and some prefer writing on a device. Some like to work alongside a counselor or life coach; others prefer going it alone. That is up to you. What is important is that you do the work.

Slowly ponder each question, even though you may choose to spend more time on some and skip others. What is essential is that you find the courage to open the box of your past and look inside it. I know you have what it takes to do this.

- What do you find challenging to think about?
- What is it you fear?

- What feelings arise when you think about those memories?

- Are there any that you feel ready to let go of?

- How might you benefit from dealing with this part of the grief?

- Will there be a cost? If so, what?

- What memories do you cherish about your loved one?

- What memories do you avoid thinking about?

- Might it be possible to bring closure to those less-than-pleasant memories?

- What aspects of your loved one's death do you need to remember?

- What aspects hinder your journey toward healing?

- If you feel any guilt, are you willing to forgive yourself?

- If you blame your loved one in any way, are you now willing to forgive them?

STEP 2

Befriending Your Past, Facing Your Grief

WRITING ABOUT MY CHILDHOOD growing up in Lampman, I realized that, for the most part, I focused on reliving the good times. There's nothing wrong with that; it can be cathartic to remember loved ones who have since passed on. But as this book is about sharing how a somewhat privileged prairie girl dealt with loss, grief, and depression, perhaps we should focus on some of those challenges. Sometimes you must go back and recognize the first times you felt anxiety and depression.

I always talk about my mom, dad, and Clinton to keep their spirits alive. I know they're gone, but that doesn't mean I can't keep them close. They will always be a part of me. Some people feel uncomfortable when you talk about those you have lost; others appreciate you sharing. Remember, these are your memories; feel free to talk about your loved ones whenever you think it will help.

Grief has a habit of making us forget, or maybe avoid, the good times and linger on the tragic day or event itself. We get stuck, and we can't move forward. Remembering our lives before losing a loved one helps put their lives and ours into perspective. A trip down memory lane can be therapeutic. My journey, tinged as it was by my feelings of sadness and loss, demonstrated how lucky I was to have shared my life with such a wonderful family and so many dear friends. I have many fond memories to hold on to, and I can share them with my children and eventually their children.

POINTS TO PONDER

Don't put expectations on yourself as to how you will grieve. I chose to write this book. Your path will likely be different.

What memories do you have from childhood where you felt alone? How did your parents or friends support you?

Think about how your mom, dad, or anyone else helped you to overcome adversity. What did it feel like? What did you learn?

- What memories would you like to relive?
- What memories are you avoiding revisiting?
- How does it feel to revisit those memories?
- Grade each memory on a scale of 1 to 10, with 1 being a memory that makes you feel distraught and

10 being a memory that makes you smile from ear to ear while feeling a warm, embracing glow.

- What, if any, lessons can you learn from those past times?

- Which childhood memories would you like to pass on to your children or loved ones?

- What qualities do you want your family or friends to know about your departed loved one?

Unlocking Trauma

LIFE WILL THROW all sorts of trauma at you; some of it will be big-*T* Trauma, the event-driven kind, but a less dramatic but also awful trauma is the type that leaves behind a slow, burning anxiety. It is deeper and more insidious; it gnaws away at you over a long period.

When a major traumatic event occurs, you will usually have access to counseling, as I did during the Shand Power Station incident; my advice is to take everything offered. The second type of trauma is trickier and is accompanied by those voices in your head that blame you or tell you there is no hope. That background narrative, that voice in your head, needs to be dealt with, and the best way to deal with it is to seek professional help.

POINTS TO PONDER

Change can be traumatic, but as long as you view it from a learning perspective, you can approach it positively. Share your concerns with friends and family, tap into your fear, and try to see how it is attempting to reframe reality. Do your best to ensure the change you are undertaking drives you toward something that will enhance your life and fill your bucket.

- Was there a time when you had to change course drastically? How did you feel when this happened?

- What did you learn about yourself in the process?

- Did you have a support system? Who out of your family and friend network supported you?

- When your life changed course, what did you learn?

- What expectations did you have about yourself when changing course?

- What was your fear telling you about the change?

- When you acknowledged that fear, how did you reframe it? In hindsight, how could you have reframed it more positively?

- What sort of things do you enjoy that are beneficial and enhance your life? How do you feel when you are doing those things?

- Are you doing what you enjoy in life? Are you living your best life? If not, what might you do to improve things?

STEP 4

Understanding Your Feelings and Emotions

TODAY, A MYRIAD of websites and forums deal with mental health issues. Information on the topic has become increasingly accessible. This openness has helped remove the stigma traditionally attached to seeking help. Of course, the big stumbling block is acknowledging that you need help in the first place.

You can cope, grief can be managed, and you will heal. In my case, I felt the most powerful tool was to recognize and understand my feelings and emotions. Realizing that you will be bombarded with negative and positive feelings is essential, as is recognizing that healing is different for everyone. I wallowed in my grief for too long; it was easier than confronting it. I self-isolated and cried for a year straight because I repressed acknowledging my feelings. I bottled them up, believing it would help me be strong. Only when I began to understand my emotions, admit to them, and embrace them did I start to heal.

Grief is a circle, not a straight line. However, I don't think one continually goes in circles; it's more like a series of twists and turns, doubling back on oneself, accompanied by feelings of déjà vu. Looking back on your grieving period, it can look more like a maze. There are so many dead ends, so many times when you don't know which way to turn, and, of course, times when you feel lost. The key is to be patient—it's a process. You need to be kind and gentle to your bruised and battered self.

Never compare your grief to that of others; your sorrow is unique to you and theirs to them. However, one thing we all have in common is the need to mourn. The challenge is that grieving is hard work; something at your core tells you to avoid the pain of the mourning process.

I didn't initially write this as a poem, but it almost felt like it needed to be written in verse.

Immediate Grief
Stunned, reeling, negative feelings.
Denial, disbelief,
Confusion, shock, sadness, yearning.
Anger, humiliation, despair, and finally, guilt,
For still being here.
Repeat.

POINTS TO PONDER

Healing cannot begin until you express how you feel; for me, this was my breakthrough moment. The day I sought help was the day that I found hope. Getting professional help was the first day of my new life. You will always grieve the death of your loved one. However, as you move forward, the grief will become less intense.

- How has your loved one's death changed you?

- Have you tried to focus on just today?

- Are you leaning on your friends and family or shutting yourself away?

- Are you able to make crucial decisions? Should you be making them, or might it be best to wait a while?

- Have you talked about your loved one? Have you considered the healing benefits of opening up?

- Are you feeling guilty? If so, about what?

- Are you showing yourself compassion? What would your loved one want for you?

- How can you shift your thinking about grief and your loved one?

- What memories of you and your loved one will you cherish for the rest of your life?

- What kind of legacy did your loved one leave behind?

- What do you want the rest of the world to know about your loved one?

- Looking back, how has grief held you back in your life?

- What have you learned about yourself during the grieving process to date?

- How can you be more present in your own life while still grieving?

Breaking the Drama Triangle

YOUR BLACK HOLE may be dark and deep, or perhaps you see or experience it in shades of gray. I hope the experiences I shared in chapter six gave you pause for thought. When you are stressed or highly anxious, try slowing everything down for a few minutes. There is no right or wrong way; just discover what works best for you. It may be as simple as listening to some music, meditating, or sitting in prayer. Think of all your stressors as being pebbles in a bucket. One by one, take them out, hold them, and turn them over in your hands for a few seconds before letting them drop to the ground. Empty your bucket one pebble and one breath at a time.

Self-help books can be a great help, but be careful which ones you choose. Check out reviews to ensure they relate to you and what you are going through. One of the first self-help books I read was *The Seven Habits of Highly Effective People* by Stephen Covey. As I'm writing this, I just took it off my bookshelf. It's probably been twenty years since I last opened its pages. My notes, underlines, and highlights leap out at me over the years, including those in the section on discovering whether our values align with our actions and if they ensure a work/life balance. I'd noted in the margin, "kids, husband, marriage." Turning the pages, I discover a series of questions and comments: "Am I really enjoying my life? Proactive people focus on what they value and care about; they are very positive. What qualities do you like about certain people in your life?" Finally: "Always have goals and write them down." I see another note written in red pen: "Some of those goals may not be met right away, be patient; it takes time."

I often get asked by people who know my story, "How did you take all that heartbreak and become who you are today?" My answer probably varies a little depending on whether I am having a good or bad day and to whom I am talking, but in essence, I tell them that there comes a time when you have grieved enough and you realize it's time to move forward. It comes when you accept life without that person.

In chapter six, I also talked about the drama triangle, so let me tell you how it became an essential tool in my life. During the time this chapter covers, we had several dental consultants and other staff in our office. Learning about the drama triangle made me aware of how I showed up in interoffice and interpersonal relationships. I would actively take sides at the time, escalating tension and drama. Sometimes, I would start gossiping behind people's backs. I craved the drama; I lived for it. Understanding the triangle allowed me to see my mistakes and how I actively played specific roles. My favorite role was the victim, because I loved people feeling sorry for me. On occasion, I would play the rescuer, because I liked the feeling of pleasing people. When I was in a bad mood, I could readily embrace the role of persecutor. To this day, I still catch myself getting sucked into the drama and then have to remind myself of the drama triangle, back off, and apologize to people. Acknowledgment is the first step. At first, it was hard for me to realize that I started a lot of the drama in my life.

I had to learn to own my behavior.

POINTS TO PONDER

- Where and how does the drama triangle show up in your relationships?
- Which role (or roles) do you play?
- Can you pick out who the players are?
- Consider how you might show up differently.
- How might you make amends if you behaved poorly in a drama?

- Knowing what you know now about the drama triangle, how could you communicate better in your relationships?

- What is important to you in your life?

- Once you discover what is important to you, does it correlate with your values?

- What expectations are you putting on yourself? Are they realistic? It's okay to recognize and accept that you are not Wonder Woman or Superman.

- What happens to you when you are overwhelmed? What feelings show up?

- Are you too hard on yourself?

- What are some ways you could show yourself compassion right now? What would that look like to you?

- How can you show others compassion, and what would that look like?

- On a scale of 1 to 10, how much do you show compassion for yourself and others?

- How can you give yourself a break?

- What does asking for support look like for you?

- How do you feel about someone else lending you a helping hand?

- How can someone else support you in different areas of your life?

Stretches, Risks, and Dies

SOMETIMES, SOMETHING dramatic—or at least cathartic—has to occur to help you change how you live your life. For some people, it's when they hit rock bottom; for others, the desire to change becomes all-encompassing. It was not until I came across the Fearless Living program that I changed my life drastically. The program gave me many tools I still use daily, more than a decade later. Here are a few to whet your appetite; I encourage you to look at the Fearless Living program or another similar program that might be better suited to how you live, or would like to live, your life.

- Ask yourself: How am I going to show up in the world?
- Ask yourself: Do I choose fear, or do I choose to live my life to the fullest?
- Write down goals and objectives to support your intentions.

Consider going on a retreat or taking an educational program—something just for you. Choose something for which you have a passion or that you feel will help you develop or increase your self-awareness. These might include programs on meditation, mindfulness, yoga, tai chi, emotional awareness, dealing with grief and loss, or discovering your hidden potential. They can allow you to get in touch with yourself and promote growth.

If you feel like tackling some of the things holding you back right now, think about an area of your life you would like to change. Then think of five things you could do that would help move you toward that change—things you've never had the confidence to do before.

These are the stretches I talked about in this chapter, and they could be as simple as sharing with a friend that you are reading this book because you think it might help you with your grief.

Now, kick it up a notch and think of a risk you might take. That could mean sitting down with your spouse, parents, siblings, or children and having an honest and open conversation about how you feel about life and your relationship with them.

Finally, think about a die you might undertake—for instance, attending a group counseling session and opening up about your loss, grief, and depression. Or maybe your die is going on that weekend retreat.

What your stretches, risks, and dies are is less important than how you begin to shift both your life and how you feel about it in a positive direction. Once you allow yourself to be vulnerable, you will grow.

POINTS TO PONDER

- Each of us has twenty-four hours each day, about nine hundred minutes of which we are awake, but only you can choose how you use your time; you can wallow in your misfortune or learn from your mistakes and live life to its fullest. The choice is yours.

- What have you learned through your grieving process so far?

- How has what you have learned served you?

- Are you willing to move out of your comfort zone to grow in self-awareness and as a person?

- Are you willing to let go so you can lessen the baggage you carry?

- What does the future hold for you? What are some things you are willing to try to manifest your desired future? Think in terms of stretches, risks, and dies.

STEP 7

Asking for Help from Others

ONE OF THE THEMES of chapter eight is that there is no right or wrong way to grieve, but as I reflect on my mother's death and how my grieving affected my relationships with other people, I can see that I could have handled my grief better, or perhaps with more awareness.

It is essential to recognize that you are not the only one grieving. It's easy to blame others for not supporting you enough, for getting on with their lives sooner than you are comfortable doing, or even for grieving differently from you. Looking back, I should have walked a mile in Keith's and my father's shoes. Maybe then I would have given them more support and less resistance.

Rather than internalizing your grief, which can be the beginning of a downward spiral, try to reach out to loved ones who are also struggling with the loss. A more positive approach might be to ask how you can support them or to simply sit down and have a conversation and communicate how you both feel. In my case, I could have made things easier by discussing with my dad how we would handle future Mother's Days instead of overreacting, especially given that it was such an important holiday for the family and had been so Mom-centric. I regret not asking how it looked for him and what would work best.

If you are grieving, avoid building a wall between yourself and the rest of your family. Take some time to think about your expectations and ask yourself, *Are they reasonable?* Are you expecting them to grieve precisely like you? I know that was what I expected of my dad. I was angry at Mom for dying—and I was angry a year later when Dad started a new relationship. It's easy to come up with silent contracts. Unfortunately, if the other person doesn't know an agreement is in place, you'll always be disappointed.

Changing how you look at things to focus on the positive instead of the negative can alter everything in a relationship. It can open the door to sharing memories of those you have lost with those who remain, rather than keeping them locked away in a mausoleum of your own making. I know one thing for sure: I missed many opportunities to build memories with my dad, and I regret that with all my heart.

I wish I had found ways to honor my mom with him as we moved past or through our grief.

POINTS TO PONDER

- Thinking you *know* how someone feels will likely damage the relationship.
- What expectations are you placing on your loved ones as you grieve and begin rebuilding your life?
- What silent contracts (unspoken agreements) do you have that hinder communication?
- Communicating your feelings is a positive step toward understanding. How can you communicate more effectively?
- What feelings must you work through before communicating with a loved one with whom you have shared a loss?
- What excuses are you making for avoiding contact with others?
- Consider the strained relationships in your life. On a scale of 1 to 10, ask yourself how meaningful each of these relationships is to you, especially now that they have become strained.

    Locking your memories in a time capsule devalues your relationship with the person you lost.

Share those memories with all of your surviving loved ones and celebrate the joy the person you lost brought to you, your family, and your friends.

Stay present in the moment. Don't get so lost in the past that you cannot honor the person you lost by living your life and moving past your grief.

Practicing Kindness and Compassion

MY FATHER HAD ALWAYS taken control of his life, but he grad-ually had that control taken from him once cancer took hold. Even when dog-tired, he fought the big *C* with extraordinary grace. And he continued to fight right up until the end.

If someone you love is dealing with cancer or any other potentially terminal disease, you may think they don't have much of a future, but help them see that what they have is today, and today matters. I asked myself how I would show up each day for myself and my father. Over the two and a half years I fought for my father's survival, I learned not to sweat the minor annoyances. To stop catastrophizing and making stuff up in my head. All that does is prevent you from living each day to its fullest. I began to find joy in the smallest moments: hearing Garrett laugh; watching Katie dance or having her show me her painting of an apple in a bowl that won first place in a the fifth-grade art competition. Dad loved that painting, so we framed it and gave it to him for Christmas.

My experience showed me the need for kindness and compassion. No one will ever judge you poorly for being too kind. Occasionally, Dad was so frustrated and scared that he would vent, and I was in the firing line. He would later say he was sorry—unnecessarily, of course.

The most important thing I learned during all of this was never to give up hope until there is no more hope. The doctors initially gave my father four months to live; I helped him live for almost two and a half years. Every day my father was alive was a gift for both of us.

POINTS TO PONDER

- What are the small joys in your life? For what are you grateful?

- What stressors prevent you from living each day to its fullest?

- Who in your life are you grateful for? Email them, text them, send them a card, or meet with them in person and tell them what they have done to help or support you and why you love them.

- Every time you interact with someone, consider what a difference you could make to their day by simply smiling or saying something nice. You'll be surprised at how good it makes you feel and the warm responses you will receive as a bonus.

- If someone you know is suffering a mental or physical illness or grieving, reach out to them and tell them how amazing they are. Sometimes a little encouragement will turn someone's day around. Write them a "just because" note. My mom and dad saved every card they ever received—I found reading them later during tough times heartwarming.

- I learned from losing Clinton, Mom, and Dad that we should never take our time on this earth for granted. If you only had one day left to live, what would you do with those twenty-four hours? How would you want to be remembered?

- Consider keeping a journal to enable you to reflect on your life. Perhaps begin by thinking about some instances where you wish you had handled things differently. How would you handle a similar situation today? Write down some of your successes and achievements. What can you celebrate?

- On a scale of 1 to 10, how much do you sweat the small stuff? Is it preventing you from fully living in the present moment? During my time with my father during his final months, I realized how easy it is to waste valuable time and energy on insignificant matters.

Step 9

Celebrating Achievements

FIND WHAT WORKS for you to keep you in the present moment. Again, it can be meditation, walking, yoga, journaling, music, or essential oils; I have even successfully tried those adult coloring books that seem so trendy these days. Anything that calms you and helps you maintain or retain control will prevent your particular version of Crazy Clyde from controlling your life. Stop wandering the dark corridors of the past, of what might have been, of what others might have done or thought, and embrace today, because today is the only reality you possess.

I encourage you to do the following exercises (I did them as part of the Choices program.) It may help you reframe your inner conversation.

- List ten times in your life when you have felt like a winner.

- Write down how you'd like people to remember you. What do you want them to remember you for? Now take it one step further, and ask yourself what would you want a *stranger* to remember about you.
  1. What do you want to accomplish before you die?
  2. List the things you have done that are important to you.

POINTS TO PONDER

- What is your purpose in life?

- What would you like to accomplish over the next five to ten years?

- How can you make a difference (e.g., with family, friends, your community, the world)?

- What have been the ten most important moments of your life?

- List ten important moments you would like to experience before you die.

- What stories do you make up in your head that are fear-based? Do you believe them?

- When you are feeling free, how do you think of yourself?

Acknowledgments

I had no idea how hard it would be to write a book, nor how incredibly rewarding and cathartic. I had to dig deep, and then deeper. The physical act of opening Clinton's trunk and going through his possessions was one of the most challenging things I have ever done. But it allowed me to move on and review my life in intense detail and tell my story.

This book would not have been possible without Mike Wicks, who encouraged me to open the trunk and have Katie film me going through Clinton's possessions. I'm eternally grateful to Mike for his unlimited patience and his ability to listen, understand, and transcribe my meandering thoughts into something I am proud of and which accurately tells my story. He has been a close confidant, life coach, writing coach, and friend. After more than two years of working together, I don't think anyone knows me better.

To my children, Garrett and Katie, for being the

inspiration to write my story and being patient with Mom when she got lost in the book.

My special thanks to Marsha; your willingness to revisit the trauma of Clinton's accident helped me fill in the missing details of that tragic time. Your friendship means the world to me.

To the Kevin Anderson and Associates team, with special thanks to editors Julia Johnson-Viola and Elizabeth Bruce and project manager Metta Sáma.

I extend my heartfelt gratitude to Kia Harris, the editorial director at my publisher, Forefront Books, and to Michael Maudlin, my developmental editor. Their unwavering support, encouragement, and publishing expertise have been invaluable in helping me bring my book to market.

Finally, to Keith, my husband, my love, my rock, for always being there for me as a sounding board and supporting me as I went back in time and revisited the many traumas of my life. Without you, I would have fallen apart years ago!

Bibliography

Rhonda Britten, *Fearless Living: Live Without Excuses and Love Without Regret,* Perigee, 2001.

Stephen Covey, *The Seven Habits of Highly Effective People,* Simon & Schuster, 1989.

Stephen B. Karpman, MD, *A Game Free Life: The Definitive Book on the Drama Triangle and Compassion Triangle,* Drama Triangle Publications, 2014.

Harriet Lerner, *The Dance of Anger: A Woman's Guide to Changing the Patterns of Intimate Relationships,* William Morrow, 1985.

Barry K. Weinhold and Janae B. Weinhold, *How to Break Free of the Drama Triangle and Victim Consciousness,* CreateSpace Independent Publishing Platform, 2013.